CAMBRIDGE LIBRARY COLLECTION

Books of enduring scholarly value

Literary studies

This series provides a high-quality selection of early printings of literary works, textual editions, anthologies and literary criticism which are of lasting scholarly interest. Ranging from Old English to Shakespeare to early twentieth-century work from around the world, these books offer a valuable resource for scholars in reception history, textual editing, and literary studies.

The Posthumous Works of Mrs Chapone

Hester Chapone (1727–1801) was a British writer and advocate of women's education who is best known as the author of one of the most popular conduct books for women in the late eighteenth and early nineteenth century. Self-educated in French, Latin and Greek, Chapone published much of her work after the death of her husband in 1761. Her firm belief in the right of women to lead emotionally and intellectually fulfilled lives was much praised by contemporary feminists. These volumes, first published posthumously in 1807, contain a biography and a series of unpublished letters from Chapone to her friends. Her letters to her friend Samuel Richardson concerning the rights of women in marriage and women's education illustrate her strong views concerning these subjects, with this volume's other letters and her biography providing further valuable insights into her character. Volume 1 contains her letters to Eliza Carter.

The Posthumous Works of Mrs Chapone

*Containing Her Correspondence with
Mr Richardson, a Series of Letters to
Mrs Elizabeth Carter, and Some Fugitive
Pieces, Never Before Published*

VOLUME 1

HESTER CHAPONE

CAMBRIDGE
UNIVERSITY PRESS

CAMBRIDGE UNIVERSITY PRESS

Cambridge, New York, Melbourne, Madrid, Cape Town, Singapore,
São Paolo, Delhi, Dubai, Tokyo, Mexico City

Published in the United States of America by Cambridge University Press, New York

www.cambridge.org
Information on this title: www.cambridge.org/9781108021722

© in this compilation Cambridge University Press 2010

This edition first published 1807
This digitally printed version 2010

ISBN 978-1-108-02172-2 Paperback

THE

POSTHUMOUS WOKKS

OF

MRS. CHAPONE.

THE

POSTHUMOUS WORKS

OF

MRS. CHAPONE.

CONTAINING

HER CORRESPONDENCE WITH MR.
RICHARDSON;

A SERIES OF LETTERS TO MRS. ELIZABETH CARTER,

AND

SOME FUGITIVE PIECES,

NEVER BEFORE PUBLISHED.

Together with

AN ACCOUNT OF HER LIFE AND CHARACTER,

DRAWN UP

BY HER OWN FAMILY.

————————

————Praising what is lost
Makes the remembrance dear.
Shakespear.

————————

VOL. I.

LONDON:

PRINTED FOR JOHN MURRAY, FLEET-STREET, AND
A. CONSTABLE AND CO. EDINBURGH.

1807.

J. WRIGHT, Printer, St. John's Square.

PREFACE.

The preface to a book may in some measure be compared to the prologue to a play, which, though it presume not to bespeak the unqualified approbation of the audience, yet tends to deprecate the mortification of severe censure.

In like manner, the editors of the following pages, though far from expecting unanimous applause, are yet willing to hope that the productions of a pen so unsullied, and the genuine display of a character so respectable as that of Mrs. Chapone, will maintain their ground on the present stage of English literature.

The custom at present prevails of publishing every relique of persons who have been in any degree eminent.— Private letters, never intended by their writers for the inspection of any,

but those to whom they were addressed,
form collections for the public eye.—
It is hoped this will plead the editor's
apology for following the taste, and
falling in with the feelings of the times.

But there are circumstances that, in
their opinion, are necessary to be stated,
because they fixed the determination to
publish these volumes.

All thoughts of printing Mrs. Chapone's correspondence with Mr. Richardson, on the subject of filial obedience, had been given up by her family,
on account of its having been suggested that the sentiments contained in
these letters were not adapted to an age
in which parental authority and filial
obedience are so much relaxed as in
the present. The few near relations
that now survive her, therefore, were
fearful of doing more injury than credit
to the fame of one, whose memory will
ever by them be held too sacred to risk

the possibility of drawing the censure of the public upon any of her writings, by an injudicious publication.

In reply to this it was urged that nothing was asserted in these letters militating against implicit filial obedience in all instances where duty to a superior authority did not interpose, and that even with respect to marriage, the parent was entitled to a negative, though not to a positive command. It was also urged, that no one could read them without recollecting they were written more than half a century ago; a period wherein many parents seemed really to suppose that parental authority extended to a right to control the affections, as well as to regulate the actions of their children; and that these letters were addressed to a person, who, both in his public writings, and (as it has been affirmed) in his private character, carried these notions to the most rigid extreme.

Feeling then the objection in a great measure, if not wholly, removed by this reasoning, the relations of Mrs. Chapone have been prevailed upon to comply with the earnest solicitations of many of her most intimate friends, and warmest admirers, in giving them to the press.

Such language and such arguments as these letters contain, can hardly fail to excite admiration, if not to afford considerable gratification in the perusal, when the reader recollects that they come from the pen of a lady, who at the age of twenty-two, with very few of the slender advantages of the education even of that moment, had discernment to detect, and courage to combat the errors of a work received with so general, nay, even enthusiastic approbation as the " History of Clarissa Harlowe."

The matrimonial creed, with the

other fugitive pieces, produced at different times, as they mark the versati-
lity of her genius, and the playfulness
of her fancy, were judged not unfit to
form a part of this little compilation.

A life, spent by choice in retirement,
is not likely to afford many anecdotes,
or furnish many events worthy of re-
cord. Such, it must be acknowledged,
was the life of Mrs. Chapone; and it
is but justice to declare that this me-
moir of it would not have been offered
to the world, had not a writing, mis-
called her life, already appeared. The
narrative here alluded to was written
without the sanction of her relations;
and published in open defiance of the
remonstrances of her friends; being
prefixed to a new edition of her " Letters on the Mind."

The only judicious part of that production is, its being so prefixed; as
that has given it a chance (which it

otherwise never could have obtained) of being read; for excepting the circumstances that she was born, that she was married to Mr. Chapone, and that she died,—it contains scarcely a single sentence that has any foundation in truth from the beginning to the end.

The immaterial circumstances guessed at, and put together in this singular piece of biography, though generally incorrect, would never have been considered as worthy of the time or trouble of notice, had not the editors, for want of information, thought fit to substitute invention for fact, and to exhibit her character in so deformed a light, that it has been deemed incumbent upon those who possessed the means, to contradict a statement by which the opinions of readers wholly unacquainted with Mrs. Chapone's character, may be so grossly misled. For they are there taught to believe, that the excellent

writer on " the government of the temper," was unable to govern her own,
and could only be ranked with the many
instances the world affords, of those
who know better how to teach than to
practise.

It has been so frequently remarked
as perhaps to require an apology for the
repetition, that the lives and characters
of persons are more faithfully delineated
in their own private letters, than in any
other mode of description. Impressed
with the truth of this observation, Mrs.
Chapone's family have been induced to
avail themselves of the kindness of the
celebrated Mrs. Eliza Carter's executor,
who has obligingly furnished them with
all Mrs. Chapone's letters to that lady;
beginning at an early age, and continued till within a year or two of her
death.

From these letters, a series of extracts has been selected, by which the

reader may be enabled to form his own
judgment of the solidity of her understanding, the vivacity of her imagination, and the affectionate tenderness of
her temper and disposition.

To these is added "a plain unvar-
nished tale" of the real circumstances
of her life, the readers of which may
rest assured that they will find nothing
in it but what is authentic, nothing
but what is strictly true. The public
will therefore, we cannot doubt, receive
it with indulgence; as designed simply
to do justice to the character of Mrs.
Chapone, to rescue it from unmerited
reproach, and preserve her memory as
it ought to be preserved, unsullied as her
life!

In these attempts, should the following work be found to succeed, the object for which it was undertaken will be
fully attained.

THE

LIFE AND CORRESPONDENCE

OF

MRS. CHAPONE.

THOMAS MULSO, Esq. of Twywell, in the
county of Northampton, the father of Mrs.
Chapone, was, at the time of her birth, the only
son of the representative of a family established
in that county before the reign of Edward
the First, and originally possessed of landed
property, in that and the adjacent counties, to
the amount of eight thousand pounds a-year;
but of which, from alienation, by means of hei-
resses, and other causes, only an inconsiderable
portion remains to the present possessor.

In the year 1719 he married the posthumous daughter of Colonel Thomas, of the guards, usually distinguished by the appellation of " the handsome Thomas."

Mr. Mulso had two sisters, the elder of whom, Anne, was married to the Rev. Dr. Donne, prebendary of Canterbury ; the youngest, Susanna, to the brother of Mrs. Mulso, the Rev. Dr. John Thomas, who was several years preceptor to his present majesty, and through the bounty of George the Second, and of his royal pupil, held successively the bishoprics of Peterborough, Salisbury, and Winchester.

Mr. and Mrs. Mulso had a numerous family of children, five only of whom lived to grow up ; and of those five, Charles, the third son, an officer in the navy, died in the Mediterranean at the age of 21.

Thomas, the eldest son, was bred to the law, and accompanied his father several years on the Oxford circuit ; but resigned all prac-

tice on coming to possession of the paternal
estate ; he was afterwards made registrar of
Peterborough, and a commissioner of bank-
rupts.

John, the second son, was a prebendary of
the cathedrals of Winchester and Salisbury,
and held two valuable livings in the county of
Hampshire.

Edward, the youngest, had a place in the
excise office, and died suddenly of an apo-
plectic seizure in April 1782.

On the respective characters of these three
brothers, it might here be thought allowable
to dwell much more at large, were it intended
that this narrative should include the life of
more than one of the family ; but although
each possessed qualities and talents well de-
serving that honourable mention should be
made of him, we shall at present confine ourselves to the avowed subject of these memoirs.

Hester Mulso, was born on the 27th of

October, 1727, and was the only daughter who reached maturity.

At a very early age she exhibited proofs of uncommon genius, and facility of apprehension. With an imagination peculiarly lively, and a temper equally warm and ardent, her young mind was more impressed and delighted by the works of fancy, than perhaps was quite consistent with due judgment, and her attachments more enthusiastic than might be compatible with her happiness.

Romances appear to have been the favourite reading of females at that period ; and it is not to be wondered at that this young lady, influenced by the example of those around her, should have read with avidity works so alluring in their composition, though so little instructive in their tendency, or beneficial in their effects. Useless, however, as such a study might have been to the generality of youthful readers, it was not wholly unproductive of advantage to her, for at nine years old she herself composed a romance,

called " The Loves of Amoret and Melissa,"
in which, though the defects of style were of
course such as would be expected from a
child of that age, such fertility of invention,
and extraordinary specimens of genius, were
displayed, as laid the foundation of that respect, and that admiration of her talents, to
which her subsequent character and writings
so fully entitled her.

Such an understanding could not long be
seduced by the absurdities of extravagant
fictions. She soon turned with disgust from
pursuits so unprofitable, and eagerly sought
every opportunity of cultivating and improv-
ing her mind.

But besides the disadvantage of living in an
age when the education of women was so
little attended to, Miss Mulso had some domestic discouragements to contend against.
Her mother, who was a woman of uncommon beauty, and whose quickness of intel-
lect was equal to her personal charms, was
not without a proportionate share of vanity,

and a consequent disposition to jealousy, naturally (or, in this instance, it may be said unnaturally) attached to that vanity. Accustomed to be almost the sole object of admiration and flattery, in whatever society she entered, she felt unwilling to relinquish any portion of that incense which she had fed upon so long.

In her daughter she found, indeed, no rival of her beauty, but she discovered a competitor in her talents, that even maternal affection did not teach her to yield to with complacency, and she was perhaps more tempted to withhold, than to bestow the assistance and instruction that she was so well qualified to afford her.

Let not this account unguardedly injure the memory of this, otherwise, really excellent woman. She had many admirable qualities to counterbalance this one unfortunate weakness ; and even for this some allowance must be made, from the excessive indulgence of an adoring husband, and a continued course of ill health, which together contributed to alter and sour a disposition originally amiable and respectable.

To the latter circumstance, indeed, may chiefly be ascribed the little attention she seemed disposed to bestow on a child who would so amply have rewarded any pains she had taken for her improvement. Her continual sufferings, in a great measure, unfitted her for the arduous task of education, and her daughter, who never failed to pay her every mark of affection and respect, was deprived of her at a time of life, when, to the generality of young women, the loss of a mother would be considered as irreparable.

From this period might be dated the commencement of the most important circumstances of Miss Mulso's life. At the same time that she took upon herself the management of her father's house, she also undertook the cultivation of her own understanding; and by dint of active exertion, and successful application, gained those mental improve-

ments that secured to her that subsequent
distinguished and admired rank in the literary
world, which she was universally acknowledged to support. Though chiefly self-
taught, she was nearly mistress of the French
and Italian languages, and even made some
proficiency in the Latin tongue.

Her studies were useful as well as elegant.
She not only read, but reflected ; and so acute
was her judgment, that no disguise of flowing
diction, or ornamented style, could mislead
it. At an age when, perhaps, few readers
are capable of very deep discrimination, she
would scrutinize and controvert every point
in which her own opinions did not acqui-
esce. That she read the Holy Scriptures
both with delight and benefit to herself, her
excellent directions for the study of them in
her letters is a sufficient testimony.

She had a turn both for poetry and philosophy; but whether it were that from the san-
guineness of her temper, she loved to look
on the bright side of every object, and con-

sequently shrank with dissatisfaction from the unpleasing picture of human nature that truth exhibited, or from some other unknown cause, certain it is she never till towards the latter part of her life, could bring herself to relish the reading of history.

She was careful to select her acquaintance amongst persons from whom she could derive profit as well as pleasure, and it was probably owing to her enthusiastic admiration of genius, and desire of seizing every possible opportunity of improvement, that she became, for a time, one of the worshippers of Mr. Richardson. But even the acknowledged authority of the celebrated writer of Clarissa could not obscure the clearness of her perception, nor check the ardour of investigation. The letters on the subject of parental authority and filial obedience, which make part of this publication, will prove with what ingenuity she could assert, and with what dignity, tempered with proper humility, she could maintain her own well-grounded opinions.

Amongst those who composed the circle of Mr. Richardson's friends, was Mr. Chapone, a young gentleman then practising the law in the Temple, for whom, from their first introduction, Miss Mulso appears to have entertained a distinguished esteem. As their intimacy improved, her attachment became rooted, and she had the gratification to perceive that it was mutual. But before Mr. Chapone had made any declaration, she felt it incumbent upon her to apprize her father of the state of her heart. He was too indulgent rigidly to discourage what prudence forbade him to approve. He exacted a promise from her, that she would not enter into any engagement without his previous permission, a promise to which she religiously adhered.

Mr. Mulso at length perceiving that their esteem for each other obviously increased upon a farther acquaintance, no longer prohibited their forming an engagement, though, from pecuniary difficulties, there was but little prospect of its concluding in a speedy union.

Miss Mulso passed this period of her life in a state of content and tranquillity, for which she never failed to express a pious gratitude, both in her conversations with, and her letters to, all her intimate friends. Excepting the circumstance of a weakly constitution, which seldom allowed her the enjoyment of full health, she had little interruption to her happiness.

She lived with a father whom she tenderly loved, and was, with his consent and approbation, frequently indulged in the society of a lover, for whom the ardour of her affection never experienced a moment's abatement, from its earliest commencement.*

* Mr. Richardson, in one of his letters, speaks of Mr. Chapone as being likely to go abroad. Whether or not he ever had such an intention, cannot now be ascertained; but certain it is, that he never did go out of England for a single day during any part of his life.

Her winters were always spent in London, in a circle of chosen and highly valued friends, amongst whom the Rev. Mr. Burrows and his sisters ranked the foremost. To this family she was indebted for some of the brightest hours of her prosperity, and on them she almost wholly reposed for comfort and kind alleviation in those of sorrow and distress, which afterwards awaited her. Indeed, it will appear in the course of this narrative, that from the small part of that family whom she had not the misfortune to survive, was chiefly derived the source of the limited share of pleasure or satisfaction that she was capable of tasting at the close of her life.

Miss Mulso, both from her natural talents and elegant acquirements, was peculiarly qualified to shine in society, and her company was coveted by all who had ever shared in the charms of her conversation. Added to the superiority her excellent understanding gave her, she was mistress of so ample a fund of humour, joined with an innate cheerfulness, as rendered her a most entertaining and desirable companion to all ages, as well as to both sexes.

Her musical talents also were such as occasioned her to be eagerly sought after by those who were lovers of real harmony. Though totally uninstructed, her voice was so sweet and powerful, her natural taste so exquisite, and her ear so accurate, that without any scientific knowledge, she would give a force of expression to Handel's compositions, that long practice, and professional skill, often failed to produce.

In summer her time was usually divided between the different country habitations of her family. Sometimes at the residence of her second brother, who was then vicar of Sunbury in Middlesex ; sometimes at the episcopal palace at Peterborough, during the time her uncle was bishop of that diocese ;*

* It is supposed the editors of the " Life of Mrs. Chapone," already published, have mistaken the bishop for Lord Peterborough, in whose house they state Miss

but more frequently at Canterbury, in the
house of her eldest aunt, Mrs. Donne, who
had been a widow some years. Here, though
in other respects it does not appear to have
been a favourite place of residence, she obtained an acquisition to her happiness, which
she cherished with partiality to the end of her
life, and considered as the chief pride and
boast of it. This was the acquaintance of
Mrs. Eliza Carter ; a lady whose fame can
admit of no addition from the efforts of so
feeble a pen, and therefore it is not intended
that an inadequate tribute of praise should be
offered to her character, but simply to speak
of her as the friend of Miss Mulso.

These young ladies seem to have been
united by mutual approbation from the moment they were first made known to each
other. Miss Mulso was then little more than
twenty, Miss Carter some years older ; and
though their sentiments were not exactly si-

Mulso to have passed some time. Neither she, nor any of
her family, ever had the honour of being acquainted with
that nobleman.

milar upon all subjects, the occasionally over-
strained imagination, and enthusiastic feelings
of the former, were so happily checked by the
solidity and deeper experience of the latter,
that probably there have existed few instances
of a friendship commenced at so early an age,
so strongly cemented, and so unalterably
continued, during a course of more than fifty
years.

Miss Carter was so engrossed by affection
and attention to her own family, and by the
extent of her literary pursuits, that no room
seems to have been left for ties of a more tender nature. This was a frequent point of
lively debate between the two friends; and
Miss Mulso, who had contracted that ardent
attachment which no impediments could dis-
solve, would humorously abuse the " square
cornered heart" of her friend, which precluded
her participating in the favourite sentiment of
her soul.

The life of Miss Mulso was now passed in a
regular routine, that furnished no incidents

to be recorded, excepting some of the early productions of her pen, which, though at the time of writing, they were solely intended for private perusal, have since been given to the public. Among the first of these were the Ode to Peace, and that addressed to her friend on her intended publication of the translation of Epictetus.

About the same time also the story of Fidelia was written ; but though composed purposely for the Adventurer, such was the timidity of the author, that nothing but the earnest persuasions of Miss Carter, and of all those friends to whose inspection she submitted it, could have prevailed upon her to take courage to send it to the press.

It would indeed have been a subject for serious regret, had this incomparable story been suppressed, which, besides the ingenuity of the invention, contains so important a lesson against the sophistry of scepticism, and exemplifies in so beautiful and touching a manner, the blessed effects of the Christian

doctrines, in language so elegant, and una-
dulterated, that those readers must be either
very weak, or incorrigibly hardened, who
could fail to be sensibly impressed by it.*

Various circumstances prevented the two
friends from spending so much of their time
together as they mutually wished ; but they
kept up a constant intercourse of writing,
which served to heighten their esteem, and to
confirm their regard for each other. Several
extracts from the letters of Miss Mulso have
been selected, which it will not be improper
to introduce in this place.

* The editors of the life before alluded to, have
thought fit to make some singular comments upon this
story; accusing it of affectation in the style, and of being
more calculated to injure than promote the cause for
which it was written. What motive they could possibly
have for so extraordinary a criticism, excepting the lite-
rally *want of something better to say*, we must leave it to
themselves to discover.

LETTER I.

September 11, 1749.

" I cannot too soon take advantage of the kind permission dear Miss Carter has given me, to begin a correspondence which will afford me so much pleasure ; and I will do it without fear, since I have as much reason to confide in her good-nature, as to revere her judgment. I shall still find in her that amiable condescension, and unreserved benevolence, which endears her conversation, and enhances the value of her understanding ; which teaches her how to improve her companions without appearing to instruct them, to correct without seeming to reprove, and even to reprove without offending.

" I parted from you, dear madam, with more regret than I dared shew ; for I could not expect that you should have believed me sincere, had I expressed all the esteem and affection I felt for you, since I could hardly, myself, comprehend how so short an acquaintance should have produced so warm an attachment : but

why do I call it a short acquaintance? I have
known you long, and long honoured and
esteemed you; but it is only since I had the
pleasure of conversing with you that I have
loved you, because fame could never have
conveyed to me any idea of the engagingness
of your manner and disposition, though it had
raised in me a just opinion of your worth and
abilities.

" I heard with great concern of your being
extremely ill after you went from Canterbury,
but had the satisfaction of hearing from Miss
——, the day before I came away, that you
were much better. I hope you are by this time
quite recovered. Are you careful enough of
your health? Yes, surely you are ; for however
deaf you may be to self-love, or however partial in your regard to your mind, in preference
to your body, yet I am certain your good-nature cannot suffer you to be insensible to the
concern of your friends, to whom your welfare is so very important."

LETTER II.

" I am extremely sorry to hear that you
have suffered so much from your own illness,
and your papa's, but hope you, by this time,
taste that additional happiness which arises
from a comparison of present ease and joy with
past pains and sorrows. I don't know whether the unspeakable satisfaction of such a reflection is not alone a sufficient compensation
for a great share of affliction, and whether
transient sufferings may not be deemed blessings in this view alone, (apart from the more
important ends which are answered by them,)
as they awaken our attention to the common
benefits we enjoy, or rather which we too often possess without enjoying, and endear those
pleasures which use had rendered too indifferent to us. The absence or sickness of our
friends enhances their value, and we receive
them, as new presents from Providence, with
redoubled tenderness and joy, when they are
restored to us. Health, which is generally
considered only as a negative happiness, becomes the source of ten thousand positive

pleasures, when it is recommended by a comparison with the languor and terrors of sickness. I hope I may congratulate you on a return of health and joy, which I am sure you will not fail to improve by reflecting properly on it. Give me leave to assure you of my sincerest good wishes for every thing that may increase or ensure your happiness.

" You are extremely obliging in the praises you bestow on my little ode. Don't accuse me of insincerity about it, for I assure you I spoke of it as I thought : you have it, however, in a less imperfect state than it was first produced in, Mr. —— having taken the pains to point out to me some of its defects, which I amended by his advice. For my own part, I was not at all inclined to take any trouble about it, had not he, with some difficulty, persuaded me it was worth mending : its correctness, therefore, (if it is correct, for that I am not qualified to judge of) you must impute to Mr. —— exactness ; an exactness which I was almost tempted to grumble at, as it put me upon

the difficulty of altering; for you, who are a
work-woman as well as a writer, know well
that it is much pleasanter to make than to
mend."

LETTER III.

January 10, 1750.

" What a wretch am I, that I must begin
every letter to dear Miss Carter with an apology! How ungrateful must I have appeared
in making no return to her kind indulgence!
Yet, as much as I want an excuse for my lazi-
ness, I can make no use of that which you
have so humbly furnished me with. You
have a right to think me a strange inconsistent
creature, but you must not think me so tasteless as not to be highly delighted with your
letters, though I have hitherto been so dilatory
in expressing the great pleasure you have given me. Your regular way of life, dear madam, whilst it is a most edifying example to
others, is far from damping your genius, or
making you less capable of entertaining, as
well as instructing, your distant friends. The

common chit-chat of the world is what one
may every where meet with, and every where
be tired with ; but where shall we meet with
the enlivened good sense, the happy mixture
of vivacity and solidity of genius and judgment which so remarkably shines in all that
Miss Carter writes ! Do not, then, impute my
silence to any but the true cause. I would
not tell you what that is, if I did not know
that you have already heard of it from Mr.——
The truth is, then, that I have been engaged
in a kind of amicable controversy with my honoured friend Mr. Richardson, which has occasioned letters of so immoderate a length between us, that I have indeed been quite tired
of pen and ink, and inexcusably negligent of
all my other correspondents. Does it not
sound strange, my dear Miss Carter, that a
girl like me should have dared to engage in a
dispute with such a man ? Don't you begin
to despise me as an arrogant, self-conceited
creature ? Indeed, I have often wondered at
my own assurance, but the pleasure and improvement I expected from his letters were
motives too strong to be resisted, and the kind

encouragement he gave me got the better of my
fear of exposing myself.

"I am going to give you a fresh proof of
my assurance, and of my dependance on your
good-nature. Mr. —— gave me the pleasure
of hearing him read the last ode you sent him,
and, miser like, I could not admire its excellence without wishing for the possession of
it ; however, I did not dare to ask him for it,
as I feared he could not comply with my request without breach of trust. May I beg the
favour of a copy from you ? and won't you
think me the boldest girl that ever lived ? Indeed I am charmed beyond measure with this
ode, and far beyond my power of praising.—
As fond as I am of the works of fancy, of the
bold imagery of a Shakespear, or a Milton, and
the delicate landscapes of Thomson, I receive
much greater and more solid pleasure from
their poetry, as it is the dress and ornament
of wisdom and morality, than all the flowers
of fancy and the charms of harmonious numbers can give,

"When gay description holds the place of sense."

Your works, my dear Miss Carter, like the
orange tree, bear flowers and fruit at the same
time, and satisfy the understanding while they
charm the imagination."

LETTER IV.

March 25.

"I was much mortified and conscience-
struck on Saturday morning, when your brother was so obliging to call on me to ask if I
would send a letter to you by him, who was
going into Kent the next day. I had not time
to write, having engagements for the whole
day, but felt myself so ashamed of not having
done it sooner, that I resolved not to let this
post go away without a letter to dear Miss
Carter, whose kind complaint of me to Mr.——
gave me pleasure and confusion at the same
time. I send you enclosed, as a peace-offer-
ing, the ode you are so obliging to ask for.
Don't think yourself obliged to praise it, but
give me your opinion of it with perfect freedom. As I don't pique myself on being a good
poetess, I shall not be hurt by being told I am

a bad one; but won't you think me a strange
variable creature, who was making resolutions
so lately never to indulge myself in scribbling
verses, and now to have the assurance to send
an ode to you, to whom I had professed those
resolutions : ' Frailty, thy name is woman !'
Perhaps the having made a resolution was
that which gave me so strong an inclination
to break it. Certain it is, that I invocated no
Muse, nor racked my brains for a thought, but
the thought came uncalled for, and the pen,
unbidden, wrote it down. My conscience
was eased of all scruples by the notable ca-
suistry of my good friend, Mr. —— who
assured me that to be better than my word was
no breach of promise. I could not help allowing the truth of his doctrine, because it suited
my inclination : so behold the fruits of it ! but
don't expose me, nor give away a copy.

" You expect, no doubt, that I should chide
you, my dear Miss Carter, for don't you deserve it, for your flagrant partiality in giving
the preference to one side of a controversy,
of which you have seen neither side ? O fie,

fie, what odd reasons indeed must those be
that could induce you to give so unfair a judgment. But I know whom to blame for it,
and I have threatened to beat him, but in vain ;
he is still partial, and would make you so ; but
don't be too much biassed by the account he
has given you of Mr. R.'s letters, which I
perceive, by what you say, has been not al-
together a just one. You say such an unmerciful prolixity upon a plain single subject,
where one is not engaged by the interesting
events of a narrative, and where there is no
room for imagery or beauty of style, is beyond
mortal sufferance ; but give me leave to assure
you that, in my humble opinion, there is great
beauty of style in many parts of Mr. R.'s letters, and that he illustrates his arguments by
a number of stories, which, (though I must
own I thought them not much to the purpose)
gave me great pleasure, from his agreeable
manner of telling them : in short, I do not believe that even you would think the time
thrown away which would be spent in reading
his part of the correspondence ; and, if I had
you in town, I would punish you for the un-

just prepossession you have entertained, by making you read it all through; then indeed I would allow you to give your opinion, and I am sure it would be a more favourable one to poor dear Mr. Richardson, who never, I believe, wrote any thing that did not shew an excellent heart and a very uncommon understanding.

"I wish I could tell you that I had any hopes of seeing you soon in Kent, but I believe I shall not be there this year, as I expect to see my aunt very soon in town. Your brother made me melancholy, by telling me that you had made something like a resolution against poor London; but then I recollected that, though a very extraordinary one, you were nevertheless a woman, and took comfort. If you defer my hopes of seeing you ever so long, I will look forward with pleasure to the prospect, however distant : the eyes of my mind are not quite so purblind as those of my body, and make nothing of looking over ten or twenty years, to find what they wish to see. Yet does not my fondness for hope prevent my

enjoying present blessings. I believe there
are few people who are better pleased and
contented with their lot than I, for I am qualified to feel my present happiness by having
early experienced very different sensations."

LETTER V.

May 18.

"And so, madam, you will laugh at me and
at my poor dear Mr. R.— why then I do pro-
test I won't bear it! Was there ever so unmerciful, so unjust, so partial a censurer! Nay,
don't wonder, for I sat down with a resolution
to scold, and I will scold, 'History of Frogs,'
'Conquest of Mexico,' 'Art of flying to the
Moon!' 'Thou hast the most unsavoury si-
milies, and art indeed the most comparative
rascally, sweet young prince!' but really and
truly, dear Miss Carter, I am half angry in
earnest at your condemning Mr. R.'s letters in
this manner, without ever having read them, and
have a great mind to send them to you in
mere spite; for after having set yourself so un-
reasonably against them, I doubt not but it

will be a punishment to you, and yet good
breeding will oblige you to read them if I send
them. Therefore pray be a little more civil,
for you see I have a way to make you repent
your unmerciful raillery. You say you honour Mr. R. but you cannot honour his prolixity ; now, seriously speaking, and partiality
laid aside, as much as I can lay it aside, I do
honour what you call his prolixity, and am
highly pleased that he has lately given us a
volume of additional letters to Clarissa.—
Things that are bad in their kind tire me, be
they but sixpenny pamphlets; but am not I
more obliged to an author who gives me three
weeks entertainment, than to him who enter-
tains me but three days? Besides, the minute
circumstances and delicate strokes and observations, which are the things that swell his
works, are, in my opinion, the principal beauties of them, and what distinguish them from
all other works of the kind I ever saw. For
my own part, I should not have quarrelled
with him for prolixity, had there been four-
teen volumes of Clarissa, provided they had
been equally beautiful with those we have

seen. As to his letters, I do not allow you to judge of them without having read them.— That they are very long I confess, nay, I will even grant that the argument would have been clearer had they been much shorter ; but there is good sense in every page, wit and humour in some, entertaining narratives in others, which narratives were not concerning the history of frogs, the conquest of Mexico, nor the art of flying to the moon ; though I have honestly owned (and thereby given you occasion to laugh, graceless as you are) that I did not think them much to the purpose of the debate between us. They are designed to prove, from the imprudencies of some individuals, how unfit young women in general are to be made independent, and how unhappy those marriages often are which are made without the advice or consent of their natural guardians and protectors. But as I never contended for any such undue liberty, as I never disputed the parents' right to a negative in the case of marriage, I do not think that any advantage could be made of these stories against me. You see that, partial as you think me, I

acknowledge my real opinion without attempt‑
ing to conceal or palliate what I think faulty.
But if you laugh at my Mr. R. I declare I
will be angry with you, for he deserves that
even his failings should be respected. And I
am very angry still (though I have vented
some of my passion) with Mr. D. for influ‑
encing you to condemn what you have never
seen. So much for scolding; and now, find‑
ing my heart eased, and my good humour re‑
turning, I will proceed, in a quiet tone, to
answer the rest of dear Miss Carter's letter.

"I am very sorry that the cause which de‑
prived me of the pleasure of hearing from you
sooner was so painful to yourself: it is great
pity that mind and body are hardly ever able
to keep even pace with each other. Your
mind should have been joined to an Herculean
body, which could have supported its share of
the fatigues of so active a companion; and
yet I am glad, for the honour of my sex, that
it was thrown into a softer form; however,
you must have some consideration for your
mortal part, and beware of bringing on your

sad head-achs, by too much or too intense study. A letter to me will cost your head no trouble, therefore I hope, untoward as you say it is, it will not refuse its consent to my being often favoured.

" Your too favourable reception of my small attempts in verse may possibly prove fatal to your repose, for should the scribbling fit ever seize me again, my maternal fondness will, in all likelihood, tempt me to send the brat to you, who seem to have so much tenderness for such poor little half-starved infants."

LETTER VI.

Peterborough, July 31.

" And so my dear Miss Carter you would have me give you an account of the new work in which Mr. Richardson is engaged ; this poor, puzzling, story-telling Mr. Richardson ! but, notwithstanding your naughty raillery, I will not punish you so severely as to forestall, and thereby lessen, the pleasure you will receive when this new work is finished, though perhaps you may think it tedious. For my own part, I cannot give it a higher commendation than to say I think it will be (if possible) superior to Clarissa; yet I must own to you that I don't believe it will be short.

" Indeed I am a little surprised that you, who are impatient with Mr. R.'s prolixity, should ever descend to the most tedious, as well as unedifying kind of reading in the world, I mean a romance. I make no scruple to call romances the worst of all the species of writing: unnatural representations of the passions, false sentiments, false precepts, false wit, false honour, and false modesty, with a strange heap of improbable, unnatural incidents mixed up with true history, and fastened upon some of the great names of antiquity, make up the composition of a romance; at least of such as I have read, which have been mostly French ones. Then the prolixity and poverty of the style is insupportable. I have (and yet I am still alive) drudged through Le Grand Cyrus, in twelve huge volumes, Cleopatra, in eight or ten, Polexander, Ibra-

him, Clelie, and some others, whose names,
as well as all the rest of them, I have forgotten ;
but this was in the days when I did not chuse
my own books, for there was no part of my
life in which I loved romances. Perhaps
those of Cervantes may be out of the common
way ; I should hardly think it possible for him
to write a book which had not in it something
admirable ; and yet I think there are one or
two very paltry novels in his Don Quixote.
I wish I was able to read the other Spanish
author, whom you mention with so much applause. Will you, in pity to us Ignoramuses,
give us, in English, a few of those passages in
which he speaks so honourably of our sex ?
Do, dear Miss Carter. We have not many
patrons amongst the men ; let us hear all that
has been said by any of the ungenerous sex in
our favour, since we are pretty sure to hear of
their abuses.

" I am very glad to hear that your health
is so much improved. I am not sorry that
you read less than you used to do, but indeed
I shall be so, if I find that you write less. I

fancy poetry is very wholesome ; it introduces
a set of pleasing images, which enliven the
spirits, and put the blood in motion. I ad-
vise you therefore, physically, to delight your
friends with now and then an ode, which
need not interrupt your walks, for I have a
notion that nothing is more proper to inspire
poetry, than a country walk in a fine evening."

LETTER VII.

Peterborough, Sept. 9.

" You give me great concern, dear Miss
Carter, when you tell me, that few years of
your life have been marked with so many
unpleasing circumstances as the past. I sincerely lament that a mind so well furnished
for happiness as yours, should be disturbed in
its self-enjoyment by the turbulence and
folly of others. There are so few people who
know how to be happy, even when every outward circumstance concurs to make them so,
that one is the less concerned when such
change their imaginary evils into real ones ;

but the unavoidable sufferings of the good and
wise ought to be every one's concern, and interest every heart in their behalf. It is indeed, as you say, vain and unreasonable to be
disappointed at finding the world what it is,
and what it must ever be on this side of the
day of doom ; and yet I find it impossible
not to be chagrined at every fresh instance of
the deceitfulness and worthlessness of the
generality of human kind. There is nothing
so painful as distrust, to a frank and honest
mind ; and yet one is perpetually feeling the
necessity of it, or suffering for the want of it.
One seldom fails to see it grow upon people
with their years, and observe that the longer
the world is known, the less it is liked, and the
less it is trusted. I am staggered and frighted
at the difficulty of hitting the true medium,
betwixt a credulity and confidence, which ex-
poses one to perpetual disappointments and
inconveniences, and a caution and distrust,
which would murder friendship, wound benevolence, and destroy all the pleasures of society. Yet I had much rather suffer by the
first, (as indeed I have more than once done)

than fall into the other most uncomfortable
extreme. Assist me, dear Miss Carter, to
avoid both, and, above all, let us both avoid a
fruitless discontent at the present state of
things, and the necessary condition of humanity; for this our sober reason will tell us
(whenever we are calm enough to hear it) is
equally painful and criminal. I think I have
insensibly fallen into a kind of preachment,
but indeed I could not know that you have
been unhappy, without being grave, and I
know you will not be disgusted with me for
being so. I hope you will tell me, in your
next, that every thing which can give you
uneasiness is removed, and that your mind
and body are both at ease, and then I know
your right disposition, and true (that is christian) philosophy, will improve that ease into
happiness.

" I am sorry you could not favour me with
a sample of Father Feyjoo's excellence. I am
a little surprised that a Spaniard should think
so favourably of women. One would imagine,
by their manner of treating them, that they

had as mean an opinion of them as the
Turks : to be consistent, every tyrant should
deny that his slaves have souls immortal like
his own.

" I am reading Doctor Young's Night
Thoughts ; I must own, with great labour both
of mind and tongue. Every word you say against
my Mr. Richardson I will revenge myself for
upon your Doctor Young. Yet I admire his
thoughts, and revere him as a philosopher and
a man ; only I cannot help lamenting that he
should have blundered so egregiously as to
fancy himself a poet. Sure never was sense
so entangled in briars as his ! Instead of the
flowers of language, his thoughts are wrapt up
in thorns and thistles. I am sure it has cost me
much toil and pain to untwist them ; and, to
say the truth, I like them as I do gooseber-
ries, well enough when they are picked for
me, but not well enough to gather them. Yet,
upon the strength of your recommendation, I
think I am resolved to go through with them,
though my tongue is already sore ; for you
must know I always read aloud here. If ever

you read one of his Nights aloud, pity my
tongue ! But, in good earnest, don't you
think he should have left off with the fourth
Night ? which I own is very fine. Don't you
think the fifth and sixth sink terribly after it ?
I am afraid you will despise me for speaking
thus of your favourite author, and, to appease
you, I will own that I think he has many extreme fine thoughts, and some few fine lines ;
but his numbers are in general so much the re-
verse of tuneful, and his language so affectedly
obscure, nay, in some places, so absolutely
unintelligible to me, that I think upon the
whole of what I have read (that is of the first
six Nights) I cannot admire the work ; but
have been oftener disgusted and tired with it
than pleased.

" I am sorry you were not at the Canterbury
races this year. I am sure I have great reason
to remember with pleasure those of last year,
where I began an acquaintance from which I
hope to receive pleasure and improvement to
the end of my life."

LETTER VIII.

London, Nov. 1%.

" I am but lately and imperfectly recovered from an illness which obliged me to have recourse to a physician. A low fever, which confined me to my chamber about a week at Peterboro', settled upon my stomach after my return to town; but the most painful, though not the most dangerous part of my disorder, was the extreme lowness and weakness of my spirits. In the depth of this vapourish state, I scribbled the Ode to Health, which I enclose to you. I hope you never saw Mr. J. D.'s on the same subject: I never did till after I had written this, and am now quite out of conceit with my own. This communication being perfectly voluntary, I would fain make a merit of it with you, in order to induce you to follow the example; but I fear you will not allow that any thing can be meritorious which is done from so selfish a motive. The other trifle Mr. D. told me you asked for.

" I am greatly pleased and edified by what you say of the disappointments we meet with from our fellow-creatures. It is, indeed, very probable that the greatest part of them proceed rather from the unjustifiable height of our own expectations, than from the artfulness and deceit of others. I am far from thinking it true, that ' a good person must necessarily be a novice ;' and allow the whole force of your observation, ' that the delicacy of virtue is more apt to be alarmed by the smallest indications of a wrong disposition, than the cunning of the wicked.' Yet I must own, to my shame, that I by no means deserve the compliment you are pleased to pay to my sagacity, of which two or three late instances have so forcibly convinced me, that all my vanity cannot keep me from being more mortified than pleased with your partial encomium. Too warm a heart, and too weak a judgment, will, I fear, often betray me into mistakes of this nature ; nor are those I have already made sufficient to preserve me from being too rashly captivated with the appearance of goodness, and, perhaps, as rashly disgusted with the first signs and marks of a disposition I dislike. It is, however, a comfort to me that I can re-

collect some instances in which the event has
justified my hasty way of judging. You
yourself are one of them, my dear Miss Carter, of whom, at first sight, I conceived an
opinion which I am sure will be more and
more confirmed the longer I live ; and for
which I will not own myself indebted to fame,
except in the articles of your understanding
and knowledge.

" In justice to myself, that you may not
think me absolutely tasteless, I think I should
tell you that I have lately read Doctor Young's
Universal Passion, and am ready to retract all
I said against him as a poet, and confine my
saucy censures entirely to that single perform-
ance of his which I cannot reconcile myself to,
the Night Thoughts. I think the four first
satires equal to any of Pope's. Those upon
women are, in my opinion, much inferior to
the others, which I hope may be accounted
for to the credit of the sex.

" I was grieved to take notice of that ser-
vile flattery, which you so justly condemn in

Doctor Young, and which is so unworthy of his character. It could never have appeared in a more shocking light than as it is introduced in a work in which the author seems to be got above the world, and almost above humanity."

LETTER IX.

" You enquire about Mr. Richardson and his new work, and I won't take it as a compliment to me that you do so. I expect you to be sincerely pleased when I tell you that this charming work goes on very fast, and will, I hope, make its appearance ere long. Mr. R. indeed sometimes talks as if it should not be published during his life; but I am very sure he will change his mind as to that particular. He can't be insensible to fame: I believe nobody that could deserve it ever was. The only objection I have to his book is, that I apprehend it will occasion the kingdom's being overrun with old maids. It will give the women an idea of perfection in a man which they never had before, and which none of the

pretty fellows they are so often fond of could
ever have furnished them with ; and the difference will be so striking between this idea and
the generality of men, that it must surely
make them nice in their choice, the consequence of which niceness will be a single life
to ninety-nine out of a hundred. I am at present in a painful uncertainty as to the catastrophe, and will not involve you in the same
uneasiness by letting you into any part of the
story. I do still think that it is, if possible,
superior to Clarissa. As I can say nothing
higher in its praise, I will not say any thing
more about it.

" Mr. —— tells me that you are a friend to
Fielding's Amelia. I love the woman, but for
the book—it must have merit, since Miss Carter and some few more good judges approve
of it. Are not you angry with the author, for
giving his favourite character such a lord and
master ? and is it quite natural that she should
be so perfectly happy and pleased with such a
wretch ? A fellow without principles, or understanding, with no other merit in the world

but a natural good temper, and whose violent love for his wife could not keep him from injuring her in the most essential points, and that in circumstances that render him utterly inexcusable. Can you forgive his amour with that dreadful, shocking monster, Miss Mathews? Are we to look upon these crimes as the failings of human nature, as Fielding seems to do, who takes his notions of human nature from the most depraved and corrupted part of it, and seems to think no characters natural, but such as are a disgrace to the human species? Don't you think Booth's sudden conversion a mere botch to save the author's credit as a moral writer? And is there not a tendency in all his works, to soften the deformity of vice, by placing characters in an amiable light, that are destitute of every virtue except good nature? Was not you tired with the two first volumes? What think you of Mrs. Bennet and her story? Pray let me have your sentiments at large on this book, for I am uneasy to know how it comes to pass that you like it, and I do not. The last volume pleased me very well; Doctor Harrison's

character is admirable; the scene between
Colonel James and his lady, excellent; that in
which Colonel James's challenge comes to the
hands of Amelia is extremely affecting; the
conversation between the Lord and Doctor
Harrison, the doctor's letter, and the comments
of the bucks upon it, I also admire very much.
And now, I think, I have mentioned all that I
can praise in the whole book; but it would
take up more paper than I have left to point
out one half of the passages that disgusted me.

" I have begun to read Guthrie's translation
of Cicero's Epistles to Atticus, and have not
been able to forbear laughing, more than once,
at the excessive vanity of your favourite Tul-
ly. You see I am in a way to deserve your
correction, and pray let me have it. I feel that
I have not so much reverence for great names
as most people have, and as, I suppose, I
ought to have. Don't spare me for this fault;
however, I am not so audacious as to deliver
these heterodox opinions to every body,
though I do to you: this may seem strange,
as I am sure there is nobody whose judgment

I revere more than yours, but I purposely lay
myself open to your reproofs, because I know
I shall benefit by them."

LETTER X.

May 27.

" It is with too much justice that dear Miss
Carter calls me a mere Vaurien ; I acknowledge myself such, nay worse ; for when people are deeply in debt, they are said to be
worse than nothing. You are so kind a cre-
ditor, that I fear there is a want of generosity
in taking advantage of your indulgence. I am
angry with myself, I hope more angry than
you are, and shall hardly be friends with myself till I am assured of your pardon.

" I am extremely obliged to you for grati-
fying my curiosity with your reasons for
speaking so favourably of Amelia, though, at
the same time, I am not a little mortified to
find that I cannot assent to all you say. I am
afraid I have less mercy in my disposition than
you, for I cannot think with so much lenity
of the character of Booth, which, though

plainly designed as an amiable one by the author, is in my opinion contemptible and wicked. ' Rather frail than wicked !' Dear Miss Carter ! that is what I complain of, that Fielding contrives to gloss over gross and monstrous faults in such a manner that even his virtuous readers shall call them frailties. How bad may be the consequence of such representations to those who are interested in the deception, and glad to find that their favourite vices are kept in countenance by a character which is designed to engage the esteem and good wishes of the reader. Had I not reason to accuse the author of ' softening or hiding the deformity of vice,' when infidelity, adultery, gaming, and extravagance, (the three last accompanied with all the aggravation that the excellence of a wife and the distress of a young family could give them) are so gently reproved, even by Miss Carter ? ' His amour with Miss Mathews,' you say, ' however blameable, was attended with some alleviating circumstances:' what these were I am unable to discover. I think none but an abandoned heart, incapable of the

least delicacy, and lost to the love of virtue
and abhorrence of vice, could have entertained any thoughts but of horror and detes-
tation for that fiend of a woman, after hearing her story. Consider too the circumstances
they were both in, Miss Mathews uncertain
whether her life was not to atone for her
crime; Booth in the deepest distress, his Amelia and her children left helpless and miserable;
a gaol the scene of their amour! What a mind
must that be, which, in such circumstances,
could find itself under any temptation from
the person of a woman whose crimes were so
shocking, whose disposition so hateful, and
whose shameless advances were so disgusting!
how mean was his submitting to owe obliga-
tions to her!—Indeed I do think him a very
wretched fellow, and I should not have cared
sixpence had the book ended with his being
hanged. In poetical justice I almost think he
should have been so. Poor Amelia would
have been rid of a good-for-nothing husband,
whose folly and wickedness gave her continual
distress. Doctor Harrison would have taken
her and her children home with him, where

I will suppose she spent her life in great tranquillity, after having recovered her fortune.—
Have not I made a fine catastrophe? Now
are you quite angry with me? I think I hear
you call me ' cruel, bloody-minded wretch!'
Well then, in complaisance to your tenderness,
I will suffer him to live, but indeed I cannot
suffer him to be a favoured character; I can't
help despising him, and wondering that Amelia did not do so too. I agree with you entirely in what you say of the mixture of virtues and faults, which make up the generality
of characters, and I am also apt to believe
that the virtues have most commonly the predominant share; but if this is the case in real
life, Mr. Fielding's representation of it is not
just; for in most of his characters the vices
preponderate. Doctor Harrison, Amelia, and
the honest serjeant are indeed exceptions;
Booth himself I cannot allow to be one, for I
do not find that he had any virtues equivalent
to his faults. Good nature, when it is merely
constitutional, and has no principle to support
it, can hardly be reckoned a virtue, and you see
that in him it was not strong enough to keep
him from injuring and distressing those he

loved best, when temptation came in his way
His regard to his wife's honour may be attri-
buted to his love ; at best it is but a negative
goodness, and only proves him not a monster.
I cannot help believing that Fielding has
a very low opinion of human nature, and that
his writings tend to enforce it on his readers ;
and I own I am always offended with writers
of that cast. What end can it serve to persuade men they are Yahoos, but to make them
act agreeably to that character, and despair
of attaining a better ! Is it not the common
plea of wicked men that they follow nature?
whereas they have taken pains to debauch and
corrupt their nature, and have by degrees re-
conciled it to crimes that simple, uncorrupted
nature would start at."

LETTER XI.

" It might perhaps be more modest in me,
dear Miss Carter, to decline your very obliging and most agreeable invitation, but
truly I am a very weak creature, and unable
to resist so strong a temptation. My aunt has

been goodnatured enough to give me her excuse and permission to leave her for a few days ; and next Friday, if convenient to you, I propose stuffing myself into that same lumbering conveyance you speak of, and embracing my dear Miss Carter between five and six in the evening. How shall I regale upon your one dish, with ' The feast of reason and the flow of soul!' Remember that you have promised me *one* dish; if I see it even *garnished* I shall take it as a rebuke for my want of modesty in taking you at your first word, and without any more ceremony making myself a part of your family. I believe indeed it is not quite right, but I can't help it, and you will see in this, as well as in an hundred other instances, when we are much together, how great an enemy I am to forms, and how dangerous it is to tempt me to any thing I have an inclination for. I have thought of nothing but being with you since I read your letter. What a sweet opportunity shall we have of knowing more of each other's minds, in three days, than we should have done in three years in the common way of visiting ! You see I take it for granted that our satisfaction is to be mutual; I believe every civil thing you say to me, and every expression of friendship from you to be perfectly sincere, without the least allowance for politeness, because I wish to believe, and because I think my dear Miss Carter is above a compliance with the fashions of the world that must cost her the smallest deviation from truth."

LETTER XII.

Canterbury, Wednesday.

" A thousand thanks to my dear Miss Carter for the happiness I enjoyed in a visit which will ever give me pleasure in reflection, though at present that pleasure is mixed with a painful regret. A thousand thanks to her for allowing me to hope a share in one of the best of human hearts, in a friendship which would do honour to the first of women, even to her Miss F——; a friendship which I can never deserve, except by the high value at which I prize it, and the sincere love and veneration with which I return it.

" I owe many thanks also to your very
agreeable sister, who seems to me to have
not only ' refined sense,' but ' all sense,'
and an excellent genius for human conveni-
ences. Though she is a wicked wit, and
laughs at me, and despises me in her heart, yet
I can't for my life be angry with her for it, but
patiently consider that ' it might have pleased
God to have made me a wit.' I saw her too
exult over me in her housewifely capacity ;—
when I folded up the gingerbread nuts so
awkwardly, I saw it was nuts to her ; but I
forgive her, and hope she will repent before
she dies of all her uncharitable insults on a
poor gentlewoman, that never was guilty of
more than four poor odes, and yet is as care-
less, as awkward, and as untidy as if she had
made as many heroic poems as the great and
majestatic Blackmore !

" You were pleased to be anxious about
my journey, therefore I must give you some
account of it. My company was much better
than I hoped, and not a man midwife amongst

them.* Imprimis, there was Mrs. ——, sister
to Mr. ——, a very sensible, well-bred old gentlewoman, who knew my aunt, and with
whom I scraped acquaintance. Item, a Mrs.
——, I think was her name, who I fancy was
one of your party at commerce, seeing she
was fat and vociferous, and looked uncommonly joyous. With her a civil gentleman-
like sort of a sail-maker, (for that he told me
was his trade) from Ratcliffe-Cross, very fat
and large, with a leg bigger than my waist.
Item, a maid servant, going to Lady ——'s,
of a middle size. Item, a very fat gentlewoman, taken up very hot at Sandwich, and set
down again at Wingham ; who, in that three
miles, with the assistance of the sail-maker,
had very near finished my journey through
this mortal life ; but her removal restored me
to the faculty of breathing, and I got to Canterbury without any casualty, save breaking
my lavender-water bottle in my pocket, and
cutting my fingers. N. B. I had like to have

* Alluding, it is supposed, to some joke of Miss Carter's.

been overturned upon Sandown, but thought of
the stoic philosophy, and did not squeak. At
Wingham we refreshed nature, and repaired
our clay tenements with some filthy dried
tongue, and bread and butter, and some well-
mixed mountain wine, by which means, as I
told you before, I was brought alive to Canterbury."

LETTER XIII.

London, Oct. 26.

"I own I am a little disappointed and
grieved to find you against me on the question between us, and still more so to be obliged to confess that I have hardly any body
of sense and experience on my side. I dare
not stand up alone in defence of mankind,
especially when my antagonists are armed
with facts which I know not how to parry or
resist. You are, however, a merciful and generous foe, and I am willing (finding my forces
so weak) to come to a composition with you.
I will grant you that there is very little virtue, and a great deal of iniquity and corrup-

tion to be found amongst those who are engaged in public life; provided you will allow
me that those are not the people in whom we
ought to look for virtue, and that human nature is not to be judged of by the most corrupted part of it. A man that is thoroughly
engaged in the pursuit of interest, and whose
principal end is the attainment of riches or
power, whatever good inclinations he might
set out with, will in all likelihood so often sa-
crifice them to his darling scheme, or at best
find so little leisure to nourish and improve
them, that in time they will languish and die,
and cease to be a part of his nature. Bad habits and artificial evil by degrees possess the
place of natural passions, and thus the man
becomes totally depraved, who perhaps set out
with an amiable benevolent mind in pursuit
of what he supposed the means of happiness,
that universal object of desire. Should we
then see him in this state of depravity, sacri-
ficing to some petty interest of his own the
interest of his country, adding to stores which
he knows no rational use for, the spoils of the
poor; persecuting with inveterate hatred the

virtue that dares to reprove or oppose him,
unattracted by the charms of innocence, and
unmoved by the tears of distress ; should we,
from his example, pronounce man to be a ma-
lign, selfish being, by nature corrupt, wicked,
malevolent ? You, my dear, have already allowed that ' mankind, as formed by the hand
of heaven, are amiable and good,' and that
' even the worst have some unconquerable
good qualities, which entitle them to some degree of tenderness and esteem.' I know not
whether any good qualities are unconquerable,
their effects at least are matters of choice, and
should not therefore, even in the worst of men,
be stript of all their merit. All our good is
certainly derived from the eternal fountain of
good, but since heaven gave it, it may be
termed our own. We are placed in a state of
warfare, surrounded with temptations and
treacherous enemies ; those who stand their
ground deserve our esteem, affection, and
applause ; and those who fall seem rather to
demand our pity than our hatred. Benevolence seems due to all ; and I cannot help being angry with all representations of human

nature which tend to weaken this divine affection, which must constitute the happiness as
well as duty of a social being. You, my dear
Miss Carter, can never be a misanthrope, the
most detestable of characters, the only one indeed which seems to justify our hatred. Human nature is still capable of exalted virtue,
and great is the number of those, who, though
they reach not the summit of perfection, are
nevertheless, in the main, good and amiable,
' innocent from the great offence,' and desirous to perform their duty. Whilst such
are easy to be found, I will not hate the world,
nor endeavour to suppress the tenderness of
my heart for every creature that wears the
human form. Private life is without doubt
the most innocent, and I will never seek
friendships out of it ; therefore I hope I shall
not be a great sufferer from the corruptions of
the grande monde, nor lose my benevolence
in the resentment of injuries. I think I read
the Rambler with great attention, yet I cannot
entirely acquit him of the charge of severity
in his satires on mankind. I believe him a
worthy, humane man, but I think I see a little

of the asperity of disappointment in his writings. You are infinitely more moderate and
merciful. I believe I almost agree to all you
have said on the subject, but my heart is averse
to a conviction which must bring with it sorrow and humiliation."

LETTER XIV.

October 11, 1752.

" I am extremely obliged to you for the
sermon : it is a most excellent one, and affected
me much. I am shocked and amazed at the
proceedings mentioned in it, and at the insolence
of Mr. ——'s ungentlemanlike letter. Well
might your excellent papa exclaim—' Hear
O Heavens and give ear O Earth.'—But
worth like his will surely in time get the better of malice, except mankind be indeed as
much depraved as the Rambler represents
them in his history of Abonaid, the son of
Morad. I own I am very unwilling to believe
those that fright us with such shocking pictures of human nature, and could almost quarrel with my very great favourite, the Rambler,
for his too general censures on mankind, and

for speaking of envy and malice as universal passions. There is, without doubt, abundance of folly and levity in the world, but I hope less malignity than the censors of it seem to suppose. Many people do mischief without designing it, and neglect to do good for want of thinking of it.

" Benevolence is often stifled and subdued by other passions, but surely it can seldom be totally extinguished or supplanted by the blackest of passions, malice. What think you my dear? am I to believe that I am surrounded with beings, who, if I am good and amiable, will hate and persecute me from envy, if frail and faulty, will rejoice in an opportunity to triumph over my weakness and to display their own superiority? who love not, but from self-interest, yet have too much pride to be capable of gratitude, and are irritated to malevolence by the burthen of benefits? Such is the human character, if we believe Mr. Johnson, and many others; who, having suffered from the world, exaggerate its faults with the bitterness of enemies, and im-

pute to the worst causes the effects by
which themselves have been hurt. It is the
commom complaint of those who have lived
long, and profess to know the world, that
young people will take no warning from their
experience, nor believe the wickedness of
mankind, till they feel the effects of it. I
should be sorry to be justly accused of such
obstinate rashness ; but yet there is something
so very uncomfortable in distrust, and in being obliged to disesteem those very creatures
whom humanity teaches us to love, that we
may surely be excused, if we are unwilling to
think so hardly of a world we have not tried,
and if we allow something for the rage of disappointment in its accusers. For my own
part, in the small circle of my acquaintance, I
find so much real merit, such exalted worth in
some, and such right intentions and harmless
inclinations in many, that, except I am to
think myself favoured beyond all other mortals
in the set of companions I am thrown into, the
world has certainly been wronged by the representation of moralists and satirists ; and
those who chuse their friends and acquaint-

ance for their worth, may find proper objects
for their best affections. But I believe many
complain that virtue is no where to be found
amongst men, who never took the trouble to
seek her, or who are not qualified for any con-
nection with her ; who chuse their friends
amongst the lightest and most profligate of
mortals, and then complain of the fickleness,
treachery, and ingratitude of the human heart.
I have another quarrel with the Rambler,
which is for the contemptuous manner in
which he generally speaks of women, for neg-
lecting to address his precepts and cautions
to them, and for drawing so many bad and ridiculous female characters, and hardly one
good one. I believe he would have found us
more docile disciples than the men, less pre-
possessed by vicious habits and passions, and
more easily attracted by the claims of virtue
and truth. I dare say you will agree with
me in this, for you carry your partiality to
your own sex farther than I do. Indeed you
have the strongest reason to think highly of it,
and have the best right of any woman in the
world to expect others to do so too.

LETTER XV.

London, Nov. 29, 1752.

" And so, my dear, in ten years time I am to subscribe to the maxim of Bias, that ' the majority are wicked !' I know not indeed how far I may be influenced by my own experience of the wickedness of a few to condemn the many, but at present I do not feel as if I could ever consent to so severe a sentence. And still less can I agree with the Rambler that malignity and envy are universal passions. On the contrary, I am persuaded that benevolence and social love (however stifled and depressed, or even sometimes totally extinguished by other passions) are originally implanted in the human breast as universally as the principle of self love, which some maintain to be the only innate affection, and the only motive of our actions. I believe I was wrong in loading the poor *little* greatones of the world with too large a share of the wickedness of it. I agree with you that those who, with smaller opportunities, are

mischievous to the worst of their power, are
equally guilty with a conqueror or a first minister. But I hope the spirit of mischief is
not so general as you seem to suppose. If
you have been a witness of some astonishing
instances of fraud, ingratitude, and malice,
you may counterbalance them by the exalted
virtues of some within the circle of your family and friends, who do honour to the human
species. Set the very good against the very
bad, and allow me to persist in thinking that
the majority are between both. Either too in-
significant to be styled virtuous, or wicked; or
else such a strange mixture of good and bad
qualities, that it is difficult to say which scale
is uppermost—are the two characters which I
fancy would be found the most general, and
under which three parts in four of mankind
should be classed. Your next paragraph delights me, for I am always pleased with myself when I find my thoughts agree with yours.
I was always offended at the assertion that the
world grows worse and worse, and that the
present age is more corrupt than all that have

gone before it. I cannot help supposing that
as the world is more enlightened, as well by the
discoveries of human reason, as by the pro-
gress of divine revelation, it is more virtuous
as well as more wise than in former ages ; and
this opinion is further justified by the flagrant
and outrageous crimes recorded in history, far
greater than any we hear of in the present
generation.

" I am but now reading Voltaire's Louis
XIV. which every body else has read long
ago. How amazing it is to me that mankind
should agree to dignify with the epithets of
great and glorious, so black a character! Yet
how if this man himself, the scourge and enemy of human kind, should have been able to
persuade himself, or suffer others to persuade
him, that he was really acting a laudable and
glorious part ! Supposing this possible, is he
not rather an object of compassion than of
hatred, and should we not rather lament human blindness, than exclaim against human
wickedness ? I am fond of this supposition,
because it saves poor Louis some part of his

guilt. Do tell me I am right, and let me fancy I have found an excuse or palliation even for a conqueror and persecutor."

LETTER XVI.

Jan. 17.

" Till the time comes when I can argue with you till you are hoarse, face to face, I must, in the spirit of tenaciousness, persecute you with arguments by letter. In the first place let me assure you that I never thought it was you ' who denied benevolence and social love to have been originally implanted in every breast;' but I thought the Rambler, whose defence you undertook, had said something like it. However, I have sufficiently harassed you on that subject, and therefore I fly to the assistance of my poor Louis, whom you would drive from every subterfuge, and rob of the poor twig I had held out, to save him from sinking into utter perdition. Seriously speaking, whether Lewis XIV. had, or had not, the excuse for his crimes which I was willing to make for him, I cannot help thinking that your argument in general proves a

great deal too much, and more than matter of
fact will justify. It proves that there can be
no such thing as innocent error, with regard
to morality ; or, in other words, that every
man has power and opportunity to know the
whole of his moral duty, which I believe is
not true in fact. You say, ' I never can believe that " the infinitely good God, should
have placed any reasonable creature in such
circumstances as to be under an impossibility
of distinguishing right from wrong, an impossibility of being virtuous, of being happy!" '

Whoever acts agreeably to the best light he
is able to obtain, and sincerely desires and in-
tends to do what is right, is virtuous, and will,
I doubt not, be happy. But that God has
placed many human beings in such circumstances as make it impossible for them to distinguish right from wrong in all cases, and
that even some of the wisest men, unassisted
by the light of revelation, are liable to mistake
in many important points of morality, is, I
think, undeniably true. It is an argument
made use of by yourself, for the necessity of

a divine revelation, that man, in his present
depraved state, is not able of himself to discover all the truths which are requisite for
him to know, in order to the regulation of his
moral conduct. And this is certainly true of
mankind in general, allowing that some few
men, of great abilities, and much leisure from
the common occupations of life, have, by slow
deductions and laborious reasoning, discovered all the great duties of morality ; and though
great part of the world is now enlightened by
the gospel, yet whole nations still remain in
darkness, whom you cannot suppose account-
able for all the immoralities which their ignorance, and the superstition they were bred up
in, makes them commit, whilst their hearts
are perhaps innocent of any evil intention.
And though this was not the case of Louis,
who must have had opportunities of knowing
the truth, yet surely some extenuation of his
crimes may be allowed, from the corruption
of flattery, and the strength the passions gain
by being continually fed and indulged. How
plausible every argument appears which coin-
cides with inclination, and how easily the un-

derstanding may be dazzled by plausibility, every one must at some period of their lives have experienced. Now, though no one can be perfectly innocent, who from indolence, or any other cause, neglects to employ the whole powers of his mind in the search of moral truth, and the detection of false arguments that tend to mislead his conduct, yet surely he who thus weakly or carelessly suffers himself to be misled, is less guilty than he who knowingly and wilfully seeks the hurt and destruction of his fellow creatures, and defies the commands of the living God. This mitigation of guilt was all I meant to plead for, with regard to poor Louis. But I think much more may be allowed for many of our fellow creatures, who, by the consequences of your argument, would stand condemned. That error may be innocent, both in faith and practice, is, in my opinion, as certain as that God is just and merciful, and will demand an account of no more than he has entrusted his servants with. That he has not made all his human creatures capable of equal perfection, is no more an imputation on his justice, than that he did not make them equal to the angels. The intention of the heart, which only the great Searcher of hearts can know, is surely that by which every individual shall be judged, and it is for this reason, I suppose, that we are repeatedly forbidden to judge and condemn one another.

" I heartily thank you for the scrap. It is an excellent introduction to the positive proofs of the truth of Christianity, which I hope you will proceed to give me."

LETTER XVII.

Hampton, July 10.

" Miss ———, who wrote to you from Northend, I suppose gave you some account of our delightful party there. How earnestly did we wish you with us. Mr. Richardson was all goodness to us, and his health being better than usual, enabled him to read and talk to us a great deal, with cheerfulness, which never appears more amiable than in him. We had a visit whilst there from your friend Mr. Johnson and poor Mrs. Williams.

I was charmed with his behaviour to her, which was like that of a fond father to his daughter. She seemed much pleased with her visit; shewed very good sense, with a great deal of modesty and humility ; and so much patience and cheerfulness under her misfortune, that it doubled my concern for her. Mr. Johnson was very communicative and entertaining, and did me the honour to address most of his discourse to me. I had the assurance to dispute with him on the subject of human malignity, and wondered to hear a man who by his actions shews so much benevolence, maintain that the human heart is naturally malevolent, and that all the benevolence we see in the few who are good, is acquired by reason and religion. You may believe I entirely disagreed with him, being, as you know, fully persuaded that benevolence, or the love of our fellow-creatures, is as much a part of our nature as self love, and that it cannot be suppressed or extinguished without great violence from the force of other passions. I told him I suspected him of these bad notions from some of his Ramblers, and had accused him to you ;

but that you persuaded me I had mistaken his sense. To which he answered, that if he had betrayed such sentiments in the Ramblers, it was not with design, for that he believed the doctrine of human malevolence, though a true one, is not an useful one, and ought not to be published to the world. Is there any truth that would not be useful, or that should not be known ?"

LETTER XVIII.

Sept. 21, 1753.

" I hope the severe sentence you pronounced upon the tender affections, ' that they never were attended with pleasures equal to half their pains,' proceeded only from the present sufferings they occasion you, and that you will soon retract it. I believe there is nothing more difficult than to make a just calculation of our pleasures and pains. The present weighs so heavy in our scale, that we can hardly do justice to the past; and pleasures more easily escape our memory than pains. Considering all this, I am willing to

hope, that the pains which attend on the social
affections are no more than a reasonable price
for the sweet pleasures that arise from them,
without which life would be insipid and uncomfortable. I allow that all excesses are de-
structive to happiness, and that the best passions may become faulty by being too much
fed and indulged. An excess of sensibility, I
believe, generally produces unhappiness ; but
yet I cannot envy the stoical heart, which is
surely in the other extreme. To practise be-
neficence without being capable of tenderness,
is perhaps most meritorious, but it is not natural, and therefore not amiable. Nothing
but affection can create affection ; and I believe no human creature is so sufficient to
himself, as to be tolerably happy without being beloved. Do not then, my dear Miss
Carter, quarrel with your heart because you
cannot make a stoic of it. Remember you are
indebted to its tenderness for your best enjoyments, and that even all your excellencies,
without that amiable quality of your nature,
could only procure you admirers, but no

friends : you would be approved and esteemed, but not beloved.

" I cannot but observe that this philosophical apathy is no where recommended to us
in the sacred writings. The laws of Christianity extend to the inward dispositions of the
heart, as well as to the outward actions; and
we are not only commanded to ' do to others
as we would they should do unto us,' but ' to
love them as ourselves.' "

LETTER XIX.

" I do not find, from my own experience,
that your philosophy is true concerning pleasures and pains, but perhaps this is owing to
the weakness or particular turn of my mind.
If you are capable of ' perpetuating the influence of agreeable circumstances,' and of
' constantly repulsing the ideas of past pains,'
you must have attained such a command over
your own imagination, as I did not suppose
possible even to you. I cannot help thinking

that pain operates more forcibly on the human mind than pleasure, and consequently leaves deeper impressions. But, on the other hand, I gratefully acknowledge that, if our pleasures are less strong, they are infinitely more numerous than our pains, and arrive in so constant and quick succession, that they leave fainter traces on the memory."

LETTER XX.

May 20,

" I am charmed with the Bishop of London's discourses. I suppose you have read them, and want to know your opinion of them, and whether you do not think them very proper to be recommended to our friend. There is such a noble freedom in his manner of thinking, and such strength and clearness in his arguments, that I think they must have weight with every unprejudiced reader. You hurt me to the heart by the doubtful manner in which you answered my question concerning my poor friend. O, Miss Carter! how unsatisfactory is every connexion we can form in

in this life, unless we can look forward to the
delightful hope of perpetuating it beyond the
grave, and of sharing together a happiness
without end or interruption! But I think
there was always a difference in our opinions
concerning the innocence of error. My own
has been much staggered by the reverence I
have for yours on all subjects of this kind; and
I have now no firm and settled opinion about
it. The merit of faith, if you confine the
sense of the word to mere belief, always appeared to me a point of great difficulty. I
wish you would give me your thoughts at
large on the subject ; particularly I would ask
wherein the merit of belief consists ? how far
is it voluntary ? and also, whether you do not
think it possible for demonstrable truths to be
proposed to a mind incapable of perceiving
the demonstration, though willing to receive
truth, and this, exclusive of the cases of lu-
nacy and folly—incapicity must of course be
innocent ? And there are circumstances which
I believe may render a person of sound understanding, incapable of sound reasoning on some
one subject ; and these circumstances may not

be matter of choice, but necessity : as for example, the strong bias of education and early
prejudices. Experience shews us how very
difficult it is to get the better of these ; and
the question with me is, whether it is even
possible to some minds to get the better of
them. When I see the strange absurdities the
human mind is capable of, and the infinite
variety of opinions that prevail amongst men,
I shudder at the thought of condemning any
person for his opinion ; and yet when I consider that opinion is that which governs all our
actions, it should seem that opinion alone con-
stitutes the man good or bad, and that on the
due regulation of our opinions depends all our
virtue, or our guilt. In short, I am lost and
bewildered in the question, and want your
guiding hand to lead me into truth."

LETTER XXI.

" I am much inclined to adopt your notion
of evil being only negative, if I could persuade myself that it would hold good on exa-
mination. But I do not find even your system

free from difficulties, and I suppose the human understanding can never form one on this subject that can give it complete satisfaction. You say, ' evil, in a certain degree, must necessarily be the lot of all created beings ;' but here you surely confound natural with moral evil. Mere defect of wisdom, which must be the lot of all created and limited intelligences, does not, I suppose, necessarily imply moral evil ; if it did, moral evil would be unavoidable, and therefore not punishable : and sin seems rather to be a wilful abuse of that portion of knowledge which is allotted us, than the mere absence of ' infallibility of wisdom.' Though all sin is folly, all folly is not sin : and I suppose that when it is said, ' he charges his angels with folly,' it is not meant that he charges them with sin ; since, according to our ideas of those happy beings, they fulfil the ends of their existence, and the laws of their nature, and are perfect in their kind, though not perfect in an absolute sense. The puzzling question is, Whence does sin derive its original ? Why should any being wilfully abuse its powers and degrade its nature, knowing that misery and ruin must be the consequence ? Why is it that even the best of us mortals must confess that though in general they love goodness, and desire to practise it, yet ' the good which they love they do not, and the evil which they would not, that they do.' What it is that can ever influence the judgment, or the will in contradiction to the judgment, to chuse evil rather than good, death rather than life, misery rather than happiness, I never could find out either in myself or other people. I cannot find out what were the motives that determined me to those actions which I have afterwards condemned, nor what it is that withholds me from constantly performing all those which I know to be right, and which I know it is in my power to perform. I shall almost make you think me running headlong into fatalism, and all manner of absurdities, but it is no such matter. I stop short in my career, and content myself with doubt and ignorance on these points ; without suffering my doubts to overturn certain clear and demonstrable doctrines, which are the rocks in which I fix my anchor, and can see the waves fluctuate about me without any great discomposure. When I have thought, and wondered, and conjectured, till I am giddy, I change the subject of my cogitations, and am as easy as if I had found out the whole scheme of Providence, in the full assurance that those things of which I am so ignorant, are adjusted exactly as they should be, and that nothing is necessary for me to know, but that which God has revealed to me."

LETTER XXII.

Sept. 27.

" How many thanks are due from me to you, my dear Miss Carter, for some of the happiest hours of my life. ' Those hours I passed with thee.' Though they are past, they have left me so rich a store for recollection, that I shall enjoy them many times over, for months to come. I can no way repay the obligation I am under to you, for bestowing your time on me in preference to so many other friends, but by telling you what I know will give you pleasure, that your visit to Canterbury has

been a great and real benefit to me. Your
conversation seems to have new set the spring
of my mind, which had been greatly hurt and
weakened. Till you arrived I was just in the
state which Miss T. so charmingly describes ;
' je mourois d'ennui !' but you have restored to
me a relish for my existence, and though you
have made me acquainted with some of the
highest pleasures this mortal state affords, you
have awakened in me the capacity of enjoying
the most common and rifling. Health and spirits returned with cheerfulness, and you my
dear were the beloved minister of all these blessings to me. Since you went I have done nothing but sing Metastatio's song. I am dis-
tracted for a tune that will go to the translation,
that I might sing that from morning till night.
Why don't Mr. Ward set it ? I have made Ned-
dy walk with me to the tree by Sir Edward
Hale's park, and intend often to reconnoitre
the spot where you sat by me there ' Io rive-
dro soventi L'amene Spiagge, O prie,' &c.

" Methinks these little romantic tendernes-
ses, these ' fond memorials,' are as natural,

and almost as pleasing, to friendship as to love.
Are you I wonder superior to all these unphilosophical indulgencies of fancy? or do the
woman and the poetess still keep their ground
against the philosopher? I believe the last is
true, and I should be sorry to find it otherwise;
if I had not observed a few dear comfortable
signs of human weakness in you, my love
would never have got the better of my reverence for you. What is the meaning I wonder
that imperfections are so attractive? and that
our hearts recoil against gigantic and unnatural excellence? It must be because perfection
is unnatural, and because the sweetest charms
and most endearing ties of society arise from
mutual indulgence to each other's failings."

LETTER XXIII.

Feb. 4, 1764.

" Mr. —— tells me, to my great concern,
my dear Miss Carter, that your ancle has not
yet recovered its strength, and that your ac_
tive spirit is still curbed and ' cramped within
a corner of the world,' instead of roaming,

like Will o' th' Wisp, over hedge and ditch,
hill and vale, through ellinge woods and barren heaths. I am afraid body and mind quarrel more than ever in this confinement. For
my part I am inclined to side with body, who
I suspect meets with hard usage from its tow-
ering mate, who seems to treat it with neglect
and disdain, as if it could hardly condescend
to acknowledge it for its partner and companion. I would as soon be Jortin's wife as your
body! and yet it has always been one of my
prayers that I might never be the wife of an
overgrown scholar.

" Methinks I am doubly audacious, in thus
declaring war at once with your mind and your
mind's favourite. Notwithstanding the compassion I feel for your body and Jortin's wife,
I have a great respect for the husbands of both;
and it is not without a degree of indignation
that I hear our admired author's remarks spoken
of with more contempt than approbation. I
own his candid freedom, and the just abhorrence he shews to every degree of persecution,
have given me a strong partiality for his work.
His wit and humour appear to me (as they are

inoffensive) very pleasing. Far unlike War-
burton's, which shocks instead of diverting
me. However, I find Jortin is censured for
his lively sallies, as being often foreign and
improper to his subject. The charge of pe-
dantry lies heavy on him, and it will be difficult to clear him from it, if it be true that
his numerous quotations from the classics answer no other purpose but that of displaying
the learning he got at school, except that of
swelling his book; and *I* may add, that of vex-
ing his unlearned readers. As to his hetero-
doxy, I do not find that any open attacks have
been made upon him, but I believe the ortho-
dox regard him as an unsound member, who,
by joining with no party, makes himself the
enemy of all."

LETTER XXIV.

April 23, 1754.

" I have been reading Leland, and had begun by Miss —— desire to write remarks on
it as I went along; but having seen hers, and
your answer, I conceived it useless for me to

go on, and have broken off in the middle, finished the book and sent it home. I am much
pleased with the work, though I have often
wished that the scheme of it had allowed a
larger scope to the answers in defence of christianity, as his references would engage one in
a dreadful long course of reading, such a one
as I am sure I shall never attempt. In general I think Dr. L—— writes with candour and
moderation, though I cannot acquit him of
deviating a little from it in some few passages.
Perhaps I am particularly nice in this respect.
All reasoners ought to be perfectly dispassio-
nate, and ready to allow all the force of the
arguments they are to confute. But more especially those who argue in behalf of christianity, ought carefully to preserve the spirit of it
in their manner of expressing themselves. I
have so much honour for the christian clergy,
that I had much rather hear them railed at,
than hear them rail, and I must say that I am
often grievously offended with the generality
of them for their method of treating all who
differ from them in opinion. I think the sum-

mary of the evidences for christianity in the conclusion, excellent.

" I believe I must quarrel with you my dear for your very unjust accusation of me with respect to roses and myrtles. Because indeed I am no florist, and cannot rattle over the names of flowers in Heathen Greek, nor have ever undertaken a journey of fifty miles to visit a tulip or an auricula, I am to be told truly that I am as well pleased with nettles as with myrtles, and that I don't know a rose from a piony! But I stoutly and resolutely deny the charge. Though I have no acquired taste for flowers, or butterflies, or china, or shells, I will say and maintain in my own behalf that nature has not denied me a nose. I have also eyes, whereby I can discern the different shapes and hues of nettles and myrtles, roses and pionies. Moreover I aver that I have often stopped my father's chair to gather May and wild woodbines from the hedges; and I well remember that in the days of my youth, when my heart was very much fixed on living in a cottage in the midst of a wood, I particularly insisted on the said cottage being covered all over with honeysuckles, and having a rose-bush on the side of the porch. And though I must confess I do not find the happiness of my life so essentially concerned in these particular circumstances now, as it was then, I am not yet fallen into the unpoetical apathy of which you so uncharitably accuse me. It is true I loved you better than flowers, and therefore stripped myself, and my aunt's little garden, to deck you with the spoils.—Ungrateful! and you to reproach me !"

LETTER XXV.

August 13.

" I ought not, I cannot, deny any request of my dear Miss Carter's which it is in my power to comply with without breach of faith to any other person, therefore I send you the verses you ask for, though I have not yet been perfectly explicit on the subject which occasioned them. I desire you will be honest and frank in giving me your opinion of them.

If you will take the pains to correct them, you
will be kinder to them than I have been, for I
never took any pains at all about them, being
fully persuaded that they would never see the
light. Whether the ode has any poetry in it
or not I can't tell, but I believe there is nature in it, because the thoughts are genuine,
and arose in my mind just in the order in
which I have set them down, in plain prose
and sober sadness. I know you will smile
at my distress with a kind of pity not much
unlike contempt, but I cannot help it, and
comfort myself with thinking, that cased up
as you are in philosophy, armour-proof against
the ' frivolous bolt of Cupid,' you will at least
forgive if not applaud me, if ever you become
intimately acquainted with the Caro Ogetto
del mio innocente ardore. Your opinion of
the lordly sex I know is not a very high one,
but yet I will one day or other make *you* confess that a man may be capable of all the delicacy, purity, and tenderness which distinguish our sex, joined with all the best qualities that dignify his own. I am very sorry to
find by your ' faint discoveries of our twilight

confidences,' that your Canterbury visit was
made so uncomfortable to you. It is odd
enough that one should find a pleasure in
talking a language that cannot be understood,
and yet it is certain that I have felt great *sou-
lagement* in giving you hints which I thought
you could make nothing out of, and that I
have been mightily gratified and wonderfully
proud of my consequence with you, when you
have in very friendly sort communicated to
me a parcel of words, whose sense remained
an absolute secret to me. How many of the
pleasures and endearments of society, as well
as the plagues and nuisances of it, arise from
little silly circumstances which reason has no
share in? This ought to make one patient
with the follies which teaze and torment us,
since we should be so loath to part with those
that please us, and upon the whole I think we
may, without any great stretch of benevolence
or philosophy, determine, that since we have
certain affections which must be disposed of
to some creature or other, it is better to bestow them on human creatures, than on antelopes or periwinkles. I think *I* may, with-

out vanity, demand a preference in your esteem, to the best periwinkle that was ever
cast on your shore. The merits of messieurs
the antelopes I am not so well acquainted
with; they may perhaps be better qualified to
be your walking mates than I am ; but in some
other qua.ities, such as hearing secrets which
I never can divulge, and contenting myself
with reasons which I don't understand, I am
sure they cannot excel me. Therefore whilst
you can have me to love, I beg you will not
make alliances with these foreigners.

LETTER XXVI.

Nov. 11, 1755.

" I know you will imagine better than I can
describe all the various sensations of my heart
on this occasion ;* for though you live among
the stoics, and study nothing but Epictetus,
you have, to my comfort, as unphilosophical a
heart as myself. What an ill-natured comfort
you will say ! Not so, my dear Miss Carter.

* An alarm about her father, who was at Bath,

The heart that is proof against pain, is inac-
cessible to pleasure ; and as I cannot help believing that the bounteous hand of Providence
has stored even this poor world with at least an
equal portion of pleasure as of pain, I have always thought it worth while to take one's share
of both. I will, however, read your Epictetus when it comes forth, and am very impatient for it, though I do not expect to be able
to adopt his maxims, or practise his doctrines.
I cannot doubt your success in any thing you
undertake, therefore I am not under any apprehensions of having my ears wounded by the
blasts of censure against your work, though I
shall be at hand to receive the first breath of
your fame. I hope and believe that you will
gain all the honour that a translation can claim.
But as that is much less than your genius is
capable of acquiring in other ways, I heartily
wish this may be the last you will ever be em-
ployed in. I do grudge you to such a task !
You ought to be an original writer, and let
your works be translated by those who can
only help the world to words, but not to new
ideas or new knowledge. Pray let me know

when you go to the press. I know you will be
in twitters, and I shall feel for you.

" But yet I rejoice that you are likely soon
to rid your hands of this laborious work, which
has so much engrossed your time, and confined your fancy. I know I speak peevishly
about it, for it always vexed me."

LETTER XXVII.

March 27, 1756.

" Most sincerely do I pity your present
situation, and heartily join in your kind wish
that I were with you ; as I flatter myself you
love me well enough to find some comfort and
relief from my sympathizing friendship. I
can easily believe that, to such a nature as
yours, scarce any circumstance could be so
irksome as that in which you find yourself,
especially as it appears that your wisdom and
benevolence have not the influence that might
be expected on the people about you. ' Epictetus would tell you this ought to give you no
concern.' I should have a great respect in-

deed for Epictetus, if he could furnish us with
a receipt to prevent our suffering any pain
from the faults and follies of those with whom
we are necessarily connected ; but if he cannot
do this, there is something very provoking in
being told that one ought not to feel. This
unreasonable precept, thank God, is but of
human authority ! The divine laws are calculated for a real, not an imaginary state of
being. They forbid the indulgence of our
natural passions and sensations, under circumstances in which they would become inju-
rious to our fellow creatures or ourselves ;
but they do not forbid the sensations themselves.

" They teach us to endure with patience,
and comfort us with the prospect of infinite
rewards ; but they do not pretend to make us
armour proof against calamity, or callous to
the feelings of humanity. How must the human understanding be distressed for want
of the revelation of a future life, when it could
only justify Providence, and maintain the
cause of virtue, by contradicting the voice of

nature, and denying the clearest evidence of
the senses! When, in order to preserve to
virtue its supposed advantages and rewards,
man was obliged, in despite of every natural
and social passion, to set up for an independent happiness, and defy his fellow mortals to
hurt him !

" And what a savage thing must be the
virtue of a philosopher! how different from
that of a christian ! Whilst the former, shut
up within himself, fancying he has found happiness in the contemplation of his own excellence, looks with proud contempt on the miseries and crimes that surround him, and stops
his ears and hardens his heart to the loud cries
of nature, who tells him, ' These whom he
despises are his brethren,' and that he himself
is every moment liable to the like distress and
the like depravity. The christian

> ' Soft and dissolving as a cloud,
> Losing itself in doing good,'

finds himself deeply interested in every thing
that concerns humanity. The fear of suffering hinders him not from making himself a

party in the affairs of others, whenever he can
hope to prevent or alleviate their misfortunes,
assist and encourage their virtue, rectify their
mistakes, sooth and mollify irritated passions,
or even afford them the consolation of being
pitied, and seeing him share in their affliction.
Their crimes and infirmities, instead of exci-
ting his hatred and contempt, alike attract his
compassion, and serve to keep awake his attention to the insecurity of his own condition,
the weakness of his own nature, and the im-
perfection of his own virtue. Humble and
diffident of himself, tender and considerate to
others, active to do good, passive and resigned to unavoidable evil, he enjoys the happiness allowed and designed for him in the exercise of the social and good affections, and,
supported by piety and hope, bears up with
cheerful fortitude under the allotted conditions
of his innocent enjoyments, pain, sorrow, solicitude, and disappointment.

" How much better qualified for the life of
man, a social and connected being, is the latter
character than the former! and how great is

our advantage, who are rescued from the inextricable maze of error, into which ignorance is plunged by pride, in following the dim light of unassisted reason! who are taught to know our true condition, our diseases and their remedies, our proper aims, our intended blessings, and our necessary sufferings! the end of our journey, and the right road through it.

" How great are our advantages! but how inexcusable the abuse or neglect of them! a fearful consideration this, my dear Miss Carter! which makes me almost tremble when I call myself a christian!

" How sweet, how amiable, and how happy (but how different from that of the stern, unfeeling philososopher!) is the disposition which we are commanded to cultivate by the blessed author of our holy religion! and how dearly (as you admirably observe) do we pay for every neglect of the wise and gracious precepts which for our own good he has enjoined us."

LETTER XXVIII.

" I am grieved to hear that you have suffered so much with the head-ache, for though
you have learnt of your friend Epictetus to
talk of the head-ache as if it were no evil, I,
who hold all that stuff in mortal contempt,
and who know you, with all your stoical airs,
to be made of nothing better than flesh and
blood like my own, am not at all comforted
by any of your jargon, nor yet, by your desir-
ing me not to concern myself about you. Till
I have learnt the art of converting my heart
into a flint, of your master Epictetus, who has
not yet been able to teach it you, I must and
will concern myself about you. And I expect
you, like an honest christian, to concern yourself about me, and to be very glad to hear
that I am wonderfully amended, and that my
spirits have been pure well for this week past,
notwithstanding a great cold, which has given
me numberless pains, and prevented my enjoying the fine weather as much as I wished.
I find myself almost as philosophical as you
about all illnesses that do not affect my spirits,

and am quite thankful and happy with a hundred aches, as long as *they* hold up and ena-
ble me to be *agreeable*."

LETTER XXIX.

Canterbury, August 29, 1757.

" Sometimes I seem, like Panthea's lover,
to have two souls. The one convinced of the
goodness of Providence ' alike in what it gives
and what denies,' cheerful and contented, and,
considering the whole of its situation, exulting
in an uncommon share of earthly happiness.
The other lamenting its incapacity to enjoy
what it has, or to attain what it wishes; en-
deavouring to account, by outward circumstances, for a depression which has its cause in
some unknown part of the body or mind, and
fancying that a change of circumstance would
make it happy; feeling pain and disgust from
objects of indifference, and indifference from
objects of pleasure. I thank God my best
soul has now the upper hand, by the assistance
of medicine and cool weather, much more
than of reason; and perhaps by the hope of

two or three days of fancied good, in the presence of a *fancied essential** to my happiness, who has promised to come down and see me some time before the middle of next month. After having been so serious, it is hardly allowable to begin again throwing stones at your poor philosopher. Yet I cannot for my life forbear hurling one at him, which I picked up t'other day out of the dirt, that is, out of Swift. ‘ The stoical method of supplying our wants by lopping off our desires, is like cutting off our feet when we want shoes.’ I was wonderfully diverted with the comparison, and immediately resolved, though I am almost barefoot here at Canterbury, not to submit to the operation, till I have tried what a certain *shoemaker at London* can do for me, who though his shoes used to pinch me at first, and gave corns, yet has now *got the length of my foot*, and fits me as well as one can reasonably expect. You see Epictetus has no great chance of getting the better of me, except he can, as the saying is, bring me down *in my wedding shoes*.”

* Mr. Chapone.

LETTER XXX.

June 20, 1758.

" I did certainly think of you very often, my dear Miss Carter, and enquire about you of every body that I thought likely to give me information ; but found all your friends hereabouts were as much in the dark about you as myself. It is however a comfort, arising perhaps from no very generous motive, to find you capable of committing the same fault, and of accounting for it in the same manner I have so often done myself. And it is a still greater comfort to have heard at last, that you are safe and well in the midst of your happy circle of friends at Deal. I was a little angry with you in my heart, when I heard of you tearing away to Deal in that violent manner the same evening that you got to Canterbury. Surely you have too little mercy on ' that paltry body of yours,' which, paltry as it is, is a good useful machine to the soul even of a philosopher, in its present state ; and should therefore be handled with less cruelty and outrage; but I know it is in vain to plead with you in its behalf, who have been always so scandalously wanting in natural affection towards it ; for my part, I cannot help loving and pitying it, for the sake of its kind offices, in bringing me acquainted with your soul ; and I own it vexes me to the heart to see it so used."

LETTER XXXI.

Canterbury, August 4.

" I am glad Mrs. H. is at Deal, for you will find some intervals to enjoy her company, and it will be of service to your spirits. My best wishes are with you, my dear friend! would I could be so myself, if I could be worth any thing to you in your present situation ! I hope, however, every day makes an alteration for the better amongst you. Providence has allotted us many resources against the long continuance of grief, if we will give way to them, as I am sure you will, and your mind is provided with materials to counteract the ill effects of that sensibility which is the

ornament and excellence of it. Do not neglect yourself in your cares for your friends,
but let medicine assist your spirits, if you
think distemper has any share in the depression you complain of. Too well I know how
long the body may suffer from the effects of
grief, after the mind is healed and restored;
take care if possible to prevent this, I conjure
you!

" I know you will be glad to hear that
I have hitherto enjoyed better health and spirits this summer, than for two or three past
summers; and am thereby enabled to keep
my very weak and unphilosophical heart in
better order than when you so justly reproved
its impatience, under circumstances that certainly ought not to be considered as serious
evils, yet which have sometimes operated on
my mind in such a manner, that I could only
cry out like the philosopher of old, ' Oh!
absence thou shalt never force me to confess
thee an evil.' Yet if pain be evil, it was certainly such to me, (through my own folly I
grant you) amidst a thousand blessings, unde-

served, and perhaps not sufficiently attended to.

" I have spent a pleasant race week, which I little expected ; but the three Miss Burrows's and a Miss Smith who is with them, came over from Margate for that week, and their company made the assemblies very agreeable to me, which would otherwise have been insufferably dull. My esteem for them increases with my intimacy ; and in spite of the caution and suspicion you and Mr. C. have taught me (and which I believe will make me very ill-natured) I am inclined to love them and approve them more than is quite consistent with my new system. Since I began to be an analyser of characters, 1 have found so few people that can please me, that I am in the more danger of attaching myself too strongly to those who can. In short, numerous are the dangers and inconveniences to which you and my other sharp-sighted friend have exposed me, by tearing off the bandage from my eyes, that so happily hid from them the bad passions and sneaking views that frequently swim within an inch of the surface of many a fair smooth-looking character. I am not however quite a misanthrope yet. You own that you are, and if such is to be the consequence of prying into the souls of one's neighbours, is it not better to employ one's understanding in considering ' whether that is possible which never did or ever will happen ?' or ' whether God loves an actually existing fly, better than a possible angel ?' "

LETTER XXXII.

" I hope your head is in good order; I was told by a gentleman t'other day, that if it was not well ballasted, it would certainly be overset by the unreasonable share of honour and praise you have gained by your late work. At the same time I was told that it had thrown the whole learned world into the utmost astonishment, and that they could no otherwise account for the thing, or comfort themselves under it, but by attributing its excellence to the archbishop's assistance. This last part of the story provokes me, but some how or other

they would fain strip the honour from our sex,
and deck out one of their own with it. I
question whether there will not be an act of
parliament next sessions to banish you this
realm, as an invader of the privileges and ho-
nours of the lords of the creation, and an occasion of stumbling to women, in the article
of acknowledging their superiority.

LETTER XXXIII.

April 28, 1759.

" I find your rambles only serve to enhance
in your esteem the beauties of Kent, towards
which you bear a truly filial partiality, as appears by the compliments you contrived to
pay it, on a comparison even with the rich
and delightful views of Berkshire. No wonder the rude scenes you are now amongst,
should be made use of as foils and contrasts to
your favoured country. However they appear
not without their charms as you have drawn
them, and I fancy you who were wont to express so high a relish of *horrible beauty*, must
find much gratification in contemplating such

an instance of the endless variety of nature.
At least it makes a fine landscape in your letter, and seems not unworthy the particular notice of your muse ; for I think the ladies of
Parnassus have no dislike to shagged grots and
barren mountains, but thrive as well amidst
such vast stupendous and horrid scenes as you
describe, as in the more flourishing, social,
and cultivated parts of the world ; at least I
am persuaded they will not refuse to follow
you, even from smiling Kent to the rough
wilds of Bristol.

" I take it for granted Mr. Johnson's Abis-
sinian Tale has reached you ; and pray tell
me whether, with all your veneration for the
author, you were not grievously disappointed
in it ? I know you have always thought me a
prophane wretch about him, as well as Doctor
Young ; but do for once give your judgment
fair play against the man's name, and tell me
whether you do not think he ought to be
ashamed of publishing such an ill-contrived,
unfinished, unnatural, and uninstructive tale ?
I know you will say there is a great deal of

good sense, and many fine observations in it.
I allow it—But how are these fine sentences
brought in ?   How do they suit the mouths of
the speakers ?   And what moral is to be drawn
from the fiction upon the whole ?   I think the
only maxim one can deduce from the story is,
that human life is a scene of unmixt wretch-
edness, and that all states and conditions of it
are equally miserable ; a maxim which, if
adopted, would extinguish hope, and consequently industry, make prudence ridiculous,
and, in short, dispose men to lie down in sloth
and despondency.   I was so well pleased with
the laudable active spirit which brought Rasselas out of the deplorable ' happy valley,'
and promised myself so fine a moral from the
superior happiness I supposed he was to find
even in hardships, wants, and dangers, when
engaged in right pursuits, to what he had experienced from the vain efforts of luxurious
idleness, that I was scandalized above measure
when I found that all his reasoning and experience were to end in his returning again to
the rattles and babies he had been tired of even
in early youth.   And that his maturity and

old age were to be spent in the balls and con-
certs he had learnt to despise soon after twenty. There is something too so strangely unnatural in drawing a young man and woman
without any one passion or predominant inclination, to determine the choice of life which
so puzzled their reason, that one cannot but
consider them as merely ideal beings, of whose
manner of feeling and acting one has no rule
by which to judge. One can as easily admit
the supposition of a ship supplied with a rud-
der and a pilot, but without either sails or oars
to set it in motion. By this time I begin to
fear you are angry with me, and consider me
as a strangely presumptuous animal, thus to
lift up my nothingness against the giant Johnson : but I think he has built too much on the
blind superstitious reverence he thinks his
name exacts from the world, and I will not be
one of those whom he will laugh at for being
taken in to admire what he must know is unworthy of him. They say he wrote it in three
mornings ; but as the Spectator says, ' I never
do excuse faults through haste.' "

LETTER XXXIV.

London, July 15, 1759.

" I allow the justice of every thing you have said relating to Mr. Johnson and his Rasselas. I own I was very angry with him for the conclusion, considering it as a conclusion, but I have since heard that he proposes going on with the story, in another volume, in which I hope he will give us antidotes for all the poisonous inferences deducible from the story as it stands at present. Alas! poor Mr. Johnson has, I fear, considered the worst side of the character of human nature, and seems to be but little acquainted with the best and happiest of its affection sand sensations. Yet, though I am scandalized and grieved at the frightful picture he has drawn of family life, I cannot but admire his truly philosophical manner of placing the advantages and disadvantages of each situation before us. Tho' I do not think he has always calculated them rightly, yet it seems to me to be the only rational *method* of considering whatever is interesting to us.

" Pray do you lead the life of a fine lady,
or do you philosophize and write even at Bristol? I am, at present, deep in stoicism; that
is to say in the Meditations of Antoninus,
which strike me with surprise and admiration,
when I consider the time, the station of the
writer, and the consonance of his life with his
principles. Pray do not you reckon him a
better natured stoic than your Epictetus? He
seems to me to be of the mildest and most sociable disposition imaginable, and not to set his
face so bitterly against human affections as I expected. His first book pleased me more than
almost any thing I ever read. I immediately
set about recollecting the different virtues and
excellencies of my friends, and the different
advantages I had reaped, or might have reaped
from each. I was not before sensible, my
dear Miss Carter, how much I was obliged to
you, amongst a few more, whom I count over
in my mind with more exultation and delight
than a miser does his bags. I could almost
have worshipped Antoninus for putting me
upon the thought, which seems to be no less
useful than pleasing. If you have not him by

heart, as I suspect you have, do read over again his first book of Reflections, and think how I crowed over it, and tell me whether there is any thing in mere human philosophy more admirable and instructive."

LETTER XXXV.

Salisbury, August 28, 1759.

" Having told you a piece of my mind concerning the way you are in, I shall now tell you something of myself, who live here uncorrupted by grandeur ; who can see venison pasties without eating them, and great dinners smoke every day without envying those whose noses are always so besmoked. Who come home from an assembly at eleven, without envying those who dance till five, and who could be content to return to my little habitation, and to that poor desart place you so much despise and hate, without envying those who live in a palace. Who could prefer a *little attorney* even to my Lord Feversham, had he offered to me instead of the fair young lady he has so happily won.

" To speak seriously though, I am happier here than at Canterbury, by many degrees, and for many reasons. The place is, I believe, the most agreeable of country towns; the people, as far as I have seen, are polite and sociable; and music is the prevailing taste amongst them—a very pleasing circumstance to me. We are a numerous family, in a noble and cheerful house; and my two young friends enliven those hours when we can escape other company. But these, alas, are few! Our grand grievance is the frequency of formal company and formal dinners, which last are, I think, amongst the worst of those many deplorable disadvantages which attend on a large fortune.

" Your friend Edward is with us, and we make a pretty little concert at home pretty often, with the assistance of the organist, and the bishop's sweet chorister, whom you heard in the Messiah, for I suppose you know *we* lent you *our* choir. Mrs. ——— (who seems to be a well bred agreeable woman) enquires after you with much regard. I know little of

Mr. ———— yet, except in his musical capacity ; but the simplicity and benevolence of
his countenance and manner charm me. I
have seen nothing yet out of the town except
Wilton, which is the most entertaining house
by way of show I ever saw, being crowded
with fine pictures, statues, busts, &c. of whose
excellence and originality being no manner of
judge, I enjoy an uncritical pleasure in be-
holding them. There is one room which I
fancy must be allowed to be the finest in England. The gardens are very pleasing, and are
nobly watered and planted. We are soon to
go to Lord Folkstone's, where, I hear, there
are a few extremely fine pictures."

The next letter announces the approach of
that important event to which Miss Mulso had
long looked forward with all the sanguine
expectation of happiness that so warm a heart
was likely to indulge.

About the end of the year 1760, Mr. Mulso,
unwilling longer to protract the union of two
of his children, so long and so unalterably at-

tached, as his daughter to Mr. Chapone, and his eldest son to Miss Prescott, arranged his affairs so as to admit of their both being married on the same day. He himself took up his abode with his son, while his daughter and her husband, as will appear by the following letters, removed first into lodgings in Carey-street, and afterwards to a house in Arundel-street.

LETTER XXXVI.

London, Dec. 9, 1760.

" My dear Miss Carter has doubtless accused me of much negligence towards her, and will probably toss down this poor despised paper as soon as she sees my hand on the cover, and debate with herself a moment whether she shall vouchsafe to read it. But after all this indignation, I know she will instantly forgive me as soon as she knows in what manner my thoughts and time have been engaged since I left Canterbury. The happiness of my own life, and that of my dearest brother, has been deeply interested in the transac-

tions of these few weeks. Thank God all is
now settled in the way we wished.

" Give me your congratulations my dear
friend ! but as much for my brother and friend
as for myself; for in truth I could not have
enjoyed my own happiness in an union with
the man of my choice, had I been forced to
leave them in the same uncomfortable state of
tedious, and almost hopeless expectation, in
which they have suffered so long.

" I shall rejoice to hear that you are coming
soon to town, and shall hope for many a comfortable *téte-à-téte* with you in my lodgings
in Carey-street; for there I must reside till
Mr. Chapone can get a house that suits him,
which is no easy matter, as he is so confined
in point of situation. In the mean time he
will carry on his business at his chambers as
before. I have therefore chosen the spot
nearest to them, though farther than I wish
from all the rest of my friends. And now let
me be no longer engrossed by selfish concerns, but enquire after your health, and that

of every one whose health is necessary to your happiness. Do not think I have forgot you, even in this time of *flutteration* ; indeed I have not ; but my time has been so much taken up, that I have hardly touched a pen since I came to town. I hope you join with me in the most perfect dissent from an opinion of your favourite Johnson, " that a married woman can have no friendship but with her husband." I flatter myself my heart will be improved in every virtuous affection by an union with a worthy man, and that my dear Miss Carter, and all my friends, will find it more worthy of their attachment, and better qualified for the best uses of friendship, than it ever was before ; at least I think it will not be less kindly disposed towards them, nor less desirous to cherish and cultivate all my valuable connexions."

LETTER XXXVII.

" I hear with great pleasure, my dear Miss Carter, that you are very soon expected in town. So I snatch up my pen in a hurry, to

put you in good humour with me before I see
you, and to tell you where you may find your
old friend, in whom you will find as much affection towards you as ever, and no one alteration, I believe, but that of name, and place
of abode. We are at present in lodgings in
Carey-street, but have taken a house in Arundel-street, both very wide from Clargis-street,
where I suppose your residence is fixed. Per-
verse thing! why are not you now in Saint
Paul's Church-yard? I ought certainly to
have thanked you sooner for your kind congratulations and good wishes. I hope, however, you will accept my thanks even now,
and consider that new-married people always
lead a life of hurry and engagement, which
leaves them little leisure or inclination for
writing letters. The drudgery of answering
all the congratulatory letters, I have put upon
Mr. Chapone, who, poor man, was forced to
humour me a little at first. Those of true
friendship, however, must not be esteemed a
drudgery. Yet I believe you can conceive it
possible to feel very averse to the thoughts of
writing, even to a friend one dearly loves.

" I dare say you had a rea. pleasure on
reading in the newspapers of the completion
of two engagements, the length of which you
had so often lamented. And I know you will
be really glad to hear, that with every other
circumstance of happiness my heart could
wish, in the beginning of a union which pro-
mises to be the best blessing of my life, I
have had the additional comfort of better
health since my marriage, than I have known
for a long time before it. Certainly ' a merry
heart does good like medicine.' Mine rejoices
almost as much for my dear brother as for myself ; God be praised, we are at present a very
happy family, and my dear good father, who
has made us so, seems to enjoy a large share
of satisfaction and pleasure in what he has
done ; his cheerfulness enabled me to bear our
parting with less pain than I expected.

" I have more hours to myself than I wish
for, for business usually allows me very little
of my husband's company, except at meals.
This I fhould be inclined to lament as an evil,
if I did not consider that the joy and complacen-

cy with which we meet, may probably by this
means last longer than if we could be always
together. If you *can* love a *man*, I expect
you will love him, if ever you know him thoroughly. In the mean time I will be contented if you love his worst half.

" His sister, who I think is a favourite with
you, is in town with the Dean of Down.
Poor Mrs. Delany set out about a fortnight
ago, on a very melancholy journey, into War-
wickshire, to attend her sister, Mrs. Dewes,
who is so ill they have but little hope of her.

" Miss Chapone always desires to be remembered to you with true esteem and respect. I am happy in having bound her to
my heart with the additional tie of sisterly
love; for she is a sweet excellent creature,
and would be a very great delight and blessing
to me, did not Mrs. Delany so often run away
with her to that ugly Ireland. I have another
new sister, whom you do not know, who is
also extremely amiable and good, but she too
is kept at a great distance from me by her

other connexions. I have a mother too, whom her son is as proud of as she is of him. But, alas, I never saw her, and God knows whether I ever shall, for she grows infirm, and her constitution has been terribly shaken by the death of a son and a husband, both within a few years. Make haste and come to town, and till then adieu, my dear friend. Believe me ever, most affectionately,

Yours,

Carey-street,   HESTER CHAPONE."
Feb. 4, 1761.

LETTER XXXVIII.

London, July 31, 1761.

" If you were ungracious in leaving town without seeing me, I have been equally so in not sooner answering your letter. So let us, my dear Mrs. Carter, exchange an act of oblivion, which I think will be better than entering into the merits of the cause on either side; for truly I think you have hardly the shadow of an excuse for not giving me the comfort of a farewel look when you were actually at my door—and I, on the other hand, might have had some excuse, had I written two or three weeks ago, my time before that, having been greatly taken up in removing into, and settling myself in, my new house. But I certainly ought to have informed you sooner, that I am at last tolerably settled, and more to my mind than I expected ; for the house, though very small, has its *agrémens*, and I don't find any ill quality in it.

" We have furnished it neatly, and the cleanliness of a house just fitted up, is not ill recommended to me by the dirt I had lived in before, in those *puddling* lodgings.

" I have just been reading Mrs. Rowe's letters from the Dead to the Living, and those called Moral and Entertaining.

" I remember you used to reproach me for not remembering them. I am extremely charmed with the first, where her luxuriant imagination has so fine a field to display itself in. But the other set of letters, which treat

of matters we are more acquainted with, seem
to me much too romantic and unnatural.

" Her descriptions of the state of the blessed
are after my own heart, and exactly suit the
rovings of my own fancy. She treats us too
with some pretty poetry, here and there, on
that subject. But her devotion is too poetical
for me, and savours too much of the extrava-
gancies of the mystics. When I hear persons
addressing the Supreme Being in the language
of the most sensual and extravagant human
love, I cannot help fancying they went mad on
a disappointment of that passion, when it was
placed more naturally. This, however, was
not Mrs. Rowe's case, for I think she was remarkably happy in marriage. I am the more
surprised that her affections broke out into
such wild torrents, since they had a free course
in their natural channel. I know she is a
great favourite of yours, and, perhaps, you
will hardly forgive this censure.—I am heartily glad you love my Burrows's, who are indeed some of the most valuable persons I
have ever known. They honour you sin-

cerely. Poor Miss Amy is still complaining,
and consequently her sisters are anxious and
unhappy. Never were four people more
strictly united in affection and friendship than
those sisters and brother. I wish you were to
hear Mr. Burrows preach. There is a simplicity and an earnestness in his manner more
affecting than any thing I ever heard from the
pulpit. His matter is not less admirable than
his manner : both seem to speak the true spirit
of christianity.

" Mr. Chapone desires his best compliments to you, though you never would
let him be acquainted with you. One very
pleasing proof of his affection for me, is, the
pleasure he takes in my friends, but I have
much ado to persuade him that you are of the
number, as he hardly ever saw us together.
' Surely, my dear,' says he, ' if Mrs. Carter
loved you, she would sometimes have spent a
day with you, and then I should have known
her better. If ever she loved you, I fancy she
has left it off on your being married.'

" This last idea seems to have taken strong possession of him, and I don't know whether I shall not be infected with the same jealousy, unless you convince me to the contrary next winter."

This was the period of her life, on which Mrs. Chapone, almost to the last hour of it, reflected, as having afforded her complete and uninterrupted happiness. Her tenderness for the lover, never experienced a moment's abatement towards the husband. She loved him with an enthusiasm that admitted not of discerning a fault in him; an affection, which, it is but justice to declare, he returned with every proof of kindness and esteem, and, during the short time their union was permitted to last, they lived together on terms of perfect harmony and mutual regard.

Always obliging and accommodating in her disposition, it cannot be questioned that she was peculiarly so to the man of her choice and the object of her fondest partiality; and the absurdity of supposing the contrary, can only be equalled by the shameless effrontery of uttering so unfounded an assertion.

The writers of the spurious production called the Life of Mrs. Chapone, in which this unpardonable falsehood is affirmed, have indeed sought shelter under high and most respectable authority, as will appear by the following sentence. " Her married life," says Mrs. Barbauld, speaking from personal observation, " was short, and not *very happy*. But in *what* this infelicity consisted, this lady has no where stated."

The reader will be pleased to take notice that the " *personal observation*" must have been the invention of the moment. Mrs. Barbauld could have been but a child at the time of Mr. Chapone's death, and was not acquainted with his widow until many years after that event.

This justly celebrated author of so many invaluable works, will feel herself but little obliged to these writers for being so kind as

to supply, from their own imaginations, what
they observe she has omitted ; and still less so,
for their obvious misconstruction of her words.
If a rumour had reached her that Mrs. Chapone was not happy in her married life, Mrs.
Barbauld certainly would not be disposed to
assign as the cause of it, Mrs. Chapone's
*" want of temper for the cultivation of domestic
tranquillity."* Her own intimate knowledge
of her heart and character must have precluded
such a supposition ; and indeed Mrs. Barbauld
has expressed, in conversation, her surprise
and concern that so unjust an accusation
should have appeared in print, and her decided opinion that it ought to be contradicted.

There yet survive one or two of her most
intimate friends, who remember Mrs. Chapone
during her married life, and can testify her
unceasing fondness for her husband, and
her invariable acquiescence in all his wishes.
Those of her nearest relations, who only remember her from a later point of time, have
been frequent witnesses of the affecting tenderness with which she spake of him, when-

ever she could assume resolution to do so ; and she preserved a miniature picture of him, which she professed that she seldom allowed herself to contemplate, because she thought it improper to indulge the sensations of exqui‑ site grief and regret it always occasioned.

The season of content which her nuptials afforded, was, however, but of short duration. In something less than ten months after they were married, Mr. Chapone was seized with a fever, which was, from the beginning, pro‑ nounced fatal, and terminated his existence after about a week's illness.

The deep distress of his afflicted wife, to‑ gether with the alarming seizure which nearly deprived her of life, the immediate conse‑ quence of this severe blow, will be best related by the following letters from her amiable and excellent friend, the eldest Miss Burrows, who hastened to town from Tunbridge, upon the first intelligence of her friend's pitiable situa‑ tion.

LETTER XXXIX.

FROM MISS BURROWS TO MRS. CARTER.

Tunbridge Wells, Sept. 17, 1761.

" MADAM,

" It is upon a very melancholy occasion I take the liberty of addressing you. Mr. Chapone has lain dangerously ill of a fever for these last ten days. The accounts we received this morning put us out of all hope of his recovery. Being well apprised of your affection for dear Mrs. Chapone, and the bad state of your spirits, we were fearful, had you first met with the account of this melancholy event in the newspaper, it might have had a bad effect upon your health; we thought it therefore most prudent to apprise you of it by this means. Our letters of to-day informed us they apprehended him dying all last night; but that she behaves with most becoming fortitude and christian patience. I dread the consequences of it upon her health in case the dreadful worst should happen; and there seems to be but little reason to flatter ourselves it will not.

" I shall go to London to-morrow, in hopes
of being some little comfort to poor Mrs. Chapone, who at present I fear is a very miserable
being. If you are desirous of further intelligence, you may command me, by directing
for me at our lodgings in Southampton-Street.
If it shall please God to give us any hopes of
Mr. Chapone's recovery, you may depend
upon hearing from me an account of it ; otherwise you may suppose the worst, for the physicians give no hopes at all. You will be comforted, I doubt not, as we are, to hear she
bears her present suspense with so much meekness and resolution.

I am, dear Madam,

Your obliged humble servant,

MARY BURROWS,"

LETTER XL.

FROM MISS BURROWS.

London, Sept. 22, 1761.

" I was very sorry your letter came so late
last night that it was impossible to answer it
by the return of the post. I am afraid the

suspense has been very painful to you. Mr. Chapone died on Saturday night, about ten o'clock. She had not been in his room since Monday last; for as her presence was judged to be very hurtful to him, she submitted to the advice of her friends not to continue her attendance upon him : she therefore was not made acquainted with his death till Sunday morning. She received the news of it with her accustomed meekness, and has, by the whole of her behaviour during his illness, and since his death, shewn an example of patience and resignation that is quite astonishing. You would hardly believe me were I to describe to you her calmness and composure, as you are so well acquainted with the strength of her passion for him. Could I tell you half the noble things she says and does, it must convince you of the sincerity of her religion, and infinitely increase your affection for her.

" Mr. and Mrs. Mulso are exceedingly friendly to her, and have kindly invited me to their house in Rathbone-Place, together with my dear afflicted friend. I told her I was going

to write to you, and she desired me to give
her kind love to you. Indeed all her friends,
and their kindness to her, are remembered by
her, particularly at this time, with so much
gratitude and affection, that it quite surprises
me, and is a pleasing mark of her gratitude
to heaven for those blessings she still pos-
sesses."

LETTER XLI.

FROM MISS BURROWS.

Oct. 5, 1761.

" As I feel myself deeply interested in the
happiness of my dear Mrs. Chapone, it gave
me a very sensible pleasure to be the bearer
of a letter so happily calculated, by its caution
as well as kindness, to convince her of your
friendship for her. I am persuaded this is a
blessing she highly esteems ; of course she was
deeply touched by this proof of your so tenderly sympathizing with her in her present
afflictions. She would herself acknowledge
the sense she has of your kindness, but her ill
state of health renders her incapable of writing

to any body. Whether this trial will not be
a greater shock to her constitution, than time,
or her resigned patient temper of mind will
be ever able to repair, is at present doubtful.
I cannot help repeating to you, that she suffers herself to be the most consoled by the
kindness of her friends I ever saw any body in
her situation : indeed, both Mr. and Mrs. Mulso are as benevolent, kind, and tender to her
as is possible. She has now a kind of inter-
mittent fever upon her, which leaves her better
in the day-time, though it never is quite off.
When she is tolerably easy she is very fond of
being read to, and is particularly delighted
with many passages in the psalms, as she finds
there her own sensations so exactly, and so
touchingly described. I wish, dear madam,
you could recommend to her any author, book,
or treatise calculated to amuse and dictate to
a mind, delicate, refined, and afflicted, as hers
is.

" I find myself quite at a loss in this search,
and therefore fly to you, well knowing (besides the more obvious reasons for such a de-

pendance upon you) your affection for her
would make any task pleasant, by which you
might procure her any present ease, or future
comfort."

" P. S. The above was written (as you will
see by the date) some days since. An acci-
dent prevented my sending it to the post immediately, and ever since poor Mrs. Chapone
has been growing worse. I have been waiting
her amendment to give you notice of it, for I
was unwilling to let you know how ill she was,
fearing the anxiety might be hurtful to you at
such a distance. I take the liberty of sending
it just as it was written, to convince you, dear
Madam, it was not without good reason I de-
tained from you the information you desired
in your last letter. She has had a pretty high
fever upon her ever since Monday last, has
suffered much in her head, stomach, and spirits, but this afternoon finds herself much better, and we all hope will get some rest, as her
fever is considerably abated. She has had
hardly any sleep for these last four nights and
days, which seemed to be an alarming circum-

stance. Though the doctor has never pronounced any immediate danger, he and all her friends have been apprehensive for the consequences of the violent restlessness that has attended her. If you desire to hear how she does, I shall with great pleasure comply with your commands, to prevent your indulging any groundless fears. I will promise to take the liberty of writing by the next post if she should be worse; so that if you hear nothing from me you may depend on her being better. I am very sorry to raise these apprehensions in your mind, but thought if I neglected writing any longer, you might justly charge me with carelessness."

" Friday night, Oct. 9."

LETTER XLII.

FROM MISS BURROWS.

October 11.

" I can now have the pleasure of informing you Mrs. Chapone is much better. The little alteration there has been in her (till within a day or two) since I wrote last, has been my

reason for not giving you any intelligence concerning her. She has had a fever constantly
every night, and been very low and dispirited
in the day : she has now been in bed twenty-
three days. I fear it is with some regret she
returns again to the world ; for had it been the
will of God, I believe she would have rejoiced
in the prospect of death, though it is not without much thankfulness she finds herself re-
leased from all her pains. She is exceedingly
low and faint, and I fear, though she should
have no unforeseen drawbacks, it will be a
long time before she recovers her strength.
The weak state she is at present in, does indeed
make her case truly pitiable."

LETTER XLIII.

FROM MISS BURROWS.

October 15.

" It is with great pleasure I can inform you
Mrs. Chapone is much better, we hope in a
fair way of recovery. We were all exceedingly alarmed about her Sunday and Monday ;
but as the doctors said it would in all proba-

bility be decided in forty-eight or twenty-four hours, I thought it was a pity to send you this melancholy account. On Monday evening she fell into a doze, and continued sleeping in an uneasy way till last night about nine o'clock. She lay quite stupid and almost insensible to every thing that passed ; when she was awake complained of being like a log ; and, in short, frightened us excessively, as we were anxiously expecting the fatal change that twenty-four hours might make in her. Thank God, this change has been in her favour, for she has had a charming night, is much refreshed by her quiet sleep, and eased of many of her pains. Her pains, indeed, have not appeared so violent for the two last days as before ; but till this morning, it seemed uncertain whether this inattention to her sufferings, was not the result of insensibility, rather than any real abatement of them.

" When she is well enough to receive it, I shall deliver your kind message, and comfort her by telling her you intend to write to her."

LETTER XLIV.

FROM MISS BURROWS.

November 11, 1761.

" I take the liberty of once more addressing you, as I imagine your solicitude for our dear friend makes a confirmation of her recovery necessary to your happiness. She has, indeed, (according to your agreeable prophecy) in a most surprising manner every day gained strength and spirits; eats heartily, and sits up all day. She thinks herself exceedingly obliged to you for your tender, friendly manner of re-membering her, as well in those letters she has received, as in those addressed to me. In-deed, madam, your friendship is a treasure she very highly prizes ; I hope it is a blessing it will please God to continue long to her.

" As soon as she is recovered enough to come out, we are in hopes of her spending a month or two at our house : heartily do I wish we could flatter her with the hopes of seeing you here, as I really believe she would be much

comforted by your conversation. May we not
hope the business you are at present engaged
in, may give us some chance for the enjoyment
of this pleasure ?

" I hope Mrs. Chapone will have the comfort of often hearing from you : it will be a
long time, I fear, before she will have the
power of writing."

These letters bear sufficient testimony of the
unalterable attachment of Mrs. Chapone to
her husband, and of the sincerity of her sorrow at his death. Contrary to the expectations of her friends, and (as will appear by the
next letter) of her own wishes, she by degrees
recovered from the dreadful illness which that
sorrow had occasioned. The following letter
to Mrs. Carter, displays her feelings and character in the most interesting point of view.
While it evinces the keenness of her sufferings,
it exemplifies the firmness of those religious
principles, which taught her so patiently to
submit to the dispensations of the all-wise dis-
poser of events.

LETTER XLV.

TO MRS. CARTER.

Southampton-street, Dec. 6, 1761.

" My dear Mrs. Carter's most kind and friendly letters, and solicitude for my welfare, claim the earliest acknowledgments in my power. Therefore one of the first uses I make of pen and ink, is to assure her of my grateful sense of it, and of the truest return of affection and friendship. I have been very near death, and at the time he threatened most, it was the most earnest wish of my heart to meet and embrace him. But I bless God I am restored not only to life, but to a sense of the great mercy indulged me in the grant of a longer term of trial. It must be my own fault if the life which is given me be not of the highest value to me, though very unlikely to be a happy one. It is, however, attended with such blessings even now, as ought to reconcile me to it. I mean particularly many kind and excellent friends, who strive as much as possible to alleviate my irreparable loss, and to supply me with every comfort I am ca-

pable of feeling. Nor are their endeavours
vain, for it has pleased God to support my
weak heart, and infirm spirits, in a wonderful
manner, even from the first of an affliction,
which I once thought it impossible for me to
survive. My illness has been a providential
circumstance in my favour. The stupidity
in which I lay some weeks, was then a happy
relief; and the natural pleasure of returning
health and strength, is now such an alleviation
of painful sentiments, that I have many cheerful hours, in which I can highly relish the
conversation of my amiable friends the Miss
Burrows's, with whom I now am on a visit
for a few weeks. I endeavour as much as possible to welcome every pleasing sensation, and
to make the most of those hours in which my
thoughts can be led from subjects of affliction.
I reckon up the treasures I have left, and
among these the friendship of my dear Mrs.
Carter is not forgotten. You are so obligingly solicitous about my circumstances, that I
would willingly inform you of the state of
them, if I had any certainty about them. But
my dear Mr. Chapone's affairs were left in

great confusion and perplexity by his sudden death, which happened just at the time of year in which he should have settled his accounts, and made out his bills. As these are very considerable, his estate must suffer a great loss from this circumstance. At present things are in a very melancholy state, and my own prospects such as would probably have appeared very dreadful to me at any other time. But the deprivation of the chief source of all my worldly happiness, has, I think, made me less sensible to other calamities."

The conclusion of this letter shews, that in addition to what she esteemed her heaviest calamity, Mrs. Chapone had some pecuniary embarrassments to encounter. This, however, was but a secondary consideration with her, nor does it ever appear to have materially affected her peace of mind. Though her circumstances no longer allowed of her keeping a house, she was content to retire upon a small, but in those days decent income, into lodgings, where she continued to make a respectable appearance.

In less than two years after the death of
Mr. Chapone, she experienced another severe
privation in the loss of her father, of which
she gives an affecting account in a letter to
Mrs. Carter, which it is not thought necessary
should appear.   He left her an addition to her
fortune, but that, in her opinion, was no compensation for the loss of so excellent and kind
a parent.

As no important occurrences took place for
several years after these events, we shall here
present all the series of extracts from her correspondence with Mrs. Carter, which it is
presumed may furnish some entertainment to
the reader.

LETTER XLVI.

July 6, 1762.

" I am grown so bad a correspondent myself, my dear Mrs. Carter, that I am very ill
entitled to the apologies you condescended to
make me, nor will I trouble you with any on
my side, as I know I may depend on your

indulgence. As this ought to be mutual, you
may assure yourself that though it is always
a very sincere pleasure to me to hear from
you, I will not even wish for it, when it would
be attended with pain or inconvenience to yourself. For my own part, writing is become so
irksome an employment to me, that were it not
the purchase of a comfort I cannot do without,
that of hearing of the welfare of my friends, I
believe I should never chuse to touch a pen.
But this, with other ill effects of bad spirits,
and a heart ill at ease, will I hope wear off in
time. I bless God I am better in all respects
than I could hope to be. Indeed I do not think
my constitution at all impaired ; on the contrary I think it is now able to sustain what in
some periods of my life would have sunk me
to the greatest weakness and dejection. How
much am I, and how much are the Miss Burrowses obliged to you, for the very valuable
and delightful acquisition you have made for
us in Mrs. Montagu's acquaintance. We all
congratulated each other, as on a piece of high
preferment, when she was so kind to invite us
to dinner the other day ; as we looked upon

it as a happy token of her inclination to admit us to something like intimacy. I begin to love her so much that I am quite frightened at it, being conscious my own insignificance will probably always keep me at a distance that is not at all convenient for loving. We had no other company at dinner except Mr. ——, a very clever agreeable man; I want to know something about his inside. Did you ever dissect his heart? or is it like another gentleman's, of whom Mrs. M. said that to look into his heart, would be to spoil one's own pleasure, like a child that breaks his plaything to see the inside of it. 'Twas a great pleasure to me to observe that Mrs. M. looked much better than when you were last in town."

LETTER XLVII.

Frith Street, Dec. 11, 1763.

" I hope your next will tell me that you are soon coming to town. We stand in great need of you and Mrs. Montagu, to produce some pleasing ideas in our minds; for London is now in such a state, that every conversation is tinctured with melancholy and horror. My friends, Miss Burrowses, reproach me often with my insensibility to public affairs, and indeed I generally am guarded, by a sanguine constitution and a most profound ignorance, from those terrors about future evils to the public, which embitter the lives of some of my acquaintance. But even I begin now to be affected with some melancholy apprehensions, and to feel myself shocked at the unbounded torrent of licentiousness which prevails every day more amongst us. Alas, how little able are we, either as a nation or as individuals, to stand the trial of great prosperity! and how constantly are outward blessings counterbalanced by internal evils! How ought this consideration to lessen our dread of calamity, and our impatience under it.

"I am much pleased to hear of Mrs.——s being a mother. I think if happiness exists here below, it must be found in her house, for her husband's letters and her own convey such ideas of it as are hardly to be met with any where else. May she never feel the loss of it! I think this last addition must complete it; for I am not

of your opinion that children are not a reasonable object of our wishes, as far as we are
permitted to wish for any temporal good. The
sensations of parental fondness are, I suppose,
the most delightful of any our nature is capable of, except the conjugal; and these mutually assist each other and complete domestic
happiness. The dangers and sorrows which
this affection often brings with it, seem to me
to shew the value of its blessings, and are no
more than the common conditions on which
we enjoy every advantage relative to this
world.

Adieu, my dear Mrs. Carter; hasten to town:
this world has nothing for me but a few friends,
and I grudge the absence of any of them.
Do not imagine from this last sentence that I
am in a state of gloom or discontent. I thank
God that is not the case. My desires of happiness are as ardent as ever. The world offers
not a shadow to content them; but the hopes
of a christian keep them from preying on the
soul, and producing that restless anxiety
which always attends them whilst any thing on

earth is their object. Yet at times a certain weariness of life, and a sense of insignificance and insipidity, deject my spirits. On such occasions I recal that beautiful thought of Milton's, in the sonnet which concludes with " They also serve who stand and wait." And then I conclude that the kindest of Beings has placed me exactly in the station fittest for me, and that it is my own fault if I do not find both occupation and enjoyment in serving him in the way he has allotted for me. Pray for me that I may do so, my dear friend, and believe me,

Ever most affectionately yours,

HESTER CHAPONE."

LETTER XLVIII.

" I learn that Mrs. Montagu is expected in town this very day, and I hope it will not be many days before I have the pleasure of seeing her, though I shall do it with an awkward consciousness about me, because my friends at Knight's tell me I ought to have written to her on the subject of her book. Could she read in my heart the true reason of my silence, it would be a higher compliment than any I could have written, for it was really no other than the high sense I have of the merit of her work, which made me despair of expressing what I thought, and ashamed of offering praise unworthy of it. As to the faults she desired me to find, she should have taken care to supply them. I am struck with beauties in every line, but do not recollect being struck with any faults, except those of the printer, which are indeed very numerous. I do most sincerely think it as elegant and brilliant a composition as I ever read ; and what particularly charms me, is the fund of good sense and sound judgment it shews, in the midst of that profusion of wit which in other works so often serves to cover a deficiency of good sense. I am told the world has been much distrest to find out the author, and has given it to some of the first wits of the other sex, little inclined to attribute the honour of it to ours. But I flatter myself it begins to be whispered all round the town, for I can't bear the thought of its being kept a secret. I have been rather

shabby of late since the wet weather came.
My enemy, Winter, begins to lay his fangs
upon me. I hate him completely now as he
does not bring my friends about me, the only
service the hideous bald-pate ever did me.
I now set all my affection on Spring, who
comes decked with snow-drops, and Carters,
and Burrowses, and such like white and lovely
virgins.

" Adieu, my dear friend : you must be very
well, for Mrs. Montagu and Mr. Pepys have
agreed to cut out work for you. They have
routed out an unknown Greek poet, who is as
precious as a Torso out of Herculaneum, and
whom you are to furbish up and translate ; so
get your head in good order."

LETTER XLIX.

Denton, August 19, 1770.

" Your last letter to Mrs. Montagu gave us
both, sufficient ease of mind to enjoy the comfort of abusing you and calling you names,
for having unmercifully kept us in anxiety so

long. After the sad account you gave of yourself in your letter to me, how came you to
forget the duty of following such an account
as quickly as possible with the news of your
recovery? Did you think we were such
" unnatural hags" as to have no concern about
you? or did you think it good for us to be
punished with fears and apprehensions about
you, whilst you were rambling about old
houses and dreaming of enchantments? Mr.
D—— too, wrote about Coal, without men-
tioning your name; however I now enjoy a
double satisfaction, in knowing you are recovered, and in having an opportunity of finding a fault in you; which is very comfortable
now and then to one who likes to be your
friend, and consequently does not like to see
you getting almost out of sight, and quite out
of reach, into the stars. I am grown as bold
as a lion with Mrs. Montagu, and fly in her
face whenever I have a mind; in short I enjoy
her society with the most perfect *gout*, and
find my love for her takes off my fear and awe,
though my respect for her character continually increases. Her talents, when consi-

dered as ornaments, only excite admiration;
but when one sees them diligently applied to every useful purpose of life, and
particularly to the purposes of benevolence,
they command one's highest esteem. I have
had no other allay to the pleasures her company gives me, and those which the variety of
scenes she has introduced me to afford, but
that of seeing her health so imperfect. Though
she has not been quite ill above two or three
times, yet she has not been well; but thank
God she is much better than she has been.
How was I delighted, my dear friend, and how
did I wish for you at Hagley! Had it not been
for Mrs. Montagu's illness there, I think I
could hardly have been more highly gratified
than by the enjoyment of that most enchant-
ing place, and of Lord Lyttelton's company.
He is always amiable, but surely never so
much as in his own house. As the weather
would not allow us to be much out of doors,
my lord consoled us by reading a good deal
of the new volume of his history. Whether it
was owing to his reading and Mrs. Montagu's
comments, or to any real superiority, I know

not; but it appeared to me still more admirable than any of the former parts of the
work."

LETTER L.

Denton, October 12.

" I am extremely sorry, my dear Mrs. Carter, to hear from Mrs. Montagu that the letter she received from you yesterday brings a
very indifferent account of your health, and
that you are confined from all enjoyment of
the fine weather. As this fine weather you
talk of, seems only an aggravation of the evil
of confinement to you, I wish you could have
imported some of it to us in the north, for our
share of sunshine has been very small. I
could have borne all the unkindness of the sky
at other times with patience, had it but smiled
upon us at Taymouth; but there its cruelty
was indeed afflicting. You have heard of our
rambles from a pen that could add even to
the beauties of the highlands; but Mrs. Montagu tells me she has left the task of description to me; a task which I can by no means

undertake : but I know I shall communicate
to you some part of my pleasure, by simply
telling you that I never enjoyed so much
from any excursion. The rude magnificence
of nature, in the degree it is displayed in
Scotland, was quite new to me, and furnished
me with ideas I never before was in possession of. At Taymouth indeed every con-
ceivable beauty of landscape is united with
the sublime. Such a lake! such variegated
hills rising from its banks! such mountains
and such cloud-cap'd rocks rising behind them!
such a delicious green valley to receive the
" sweet winding Tay!" such woods! such
cascades!—in short I am wild that you and
all my romantic friends should see it ; for even
a Milton's pen, or a Salvator Rosa's pencil,
would fail to give you a complete idea of it.
Several more sweet places we saw, which
would have made capital figures, had they
not been eclipsed by Lord Bredalbane's. My
intellectual pleasures were as great in their
kind, from the conversations of Mrs. Montagu
and Dr. Gregory, who accompanied us in all
our journeys, and is one of the most agreeable

men I ever met with. Many other personages of note were drawn together by the magnetism of Mrs. Montagu at Edinburgh.

There is great pleasure you know in seeing live authors, which makes me regret that David Hume could not come to the meeting. Dr. Robertson we saw a good deal of: I like him well. The greatest pleasure I derive from this journey, which has afforded me so much, is that of seeing Mrs. Montagu in a much more comfortable state of health than before; and in a way, I hope, to receive lasting benefit from the course into which her Scotch physicians have put her, which is different from all that was tried before; and hitherto it has certainly agreed with her. She talks of moving southward the beginning of the week after next; and I shall be sorry if she is obliged to defer it longer, for I think neither she nor I are well qualified for a winter journey of such length.

" I am much obliged to you for sending Mrs. ——'s paper to Lady Dartry, and for your kind intention of bringing me acquainted with her. I can have no doubt of the value of an acquaintance with a person you esteem so much, but have great doubt of answering the expectations your partial friendship may have raised. However that prove, I shall certainly think myself much honoured by her notice. I am a little afraid that the advantage of your's and Mrs. Montagu's kind opinion of me, will enlarge my acquaintance more than is consistent with my manner of living in town. It will be necessary for me to guard against this, though, in other circumstances, nothing could be more desirable than the acquisition of such acquaintance as your circle affords, and on whose account Mr. Burrows rejoices that he never, in any of his sermons, launched out into any common place against the rich and great."

LETTER LI.

Farnham Castle, Sept. 21.

" You will hardly believe, my dear Mrs. Carter, how often I think of you, and how often I have wished and intended to thank you

for your last most kind letter, which I received
just before I left London : but the difficulty of
getting time enough to myself to write a letter
here, cannot be conceived by any one who
has not been in the situation. My thoughts
however are free, and they have often dwelt
on you, and on the candour and friendship expressed in your letter. I entirely agree with
you on the justice of your severity towards
those, who, to gratify their own vanity, destroy
the principles, and consequently the happiness
of their fellow-creatures. If the infidel writers
act on such motives, and see the consequences
of what they do, they are without excuse,
and ought to be detested as the enemies of
human-kind. Nor did your just resentment
against them, ever lead me to suspect you of
being deficient in candour towards innocent
error, or modest doubtfulness. Of this I have
given you proofs, and you on your side have
confirmed my affiance in you in the kindest
manner. Since I wrote to you last, I have
read five volumes of Lardner's Credibility of
the Gospel History, which I think affords sufficient proof that the canon of scripture re-

ceived by us, is the same that was received in
the earliest ages of christianity, and that the
spurious ones were never accepted in those
ages, except by a few schismatics. This certainly is a good foundation to build other
proofs upon. I have read Mrs. Scott's life of
D'Aubigné with much pleasure, and think
the style much superior to any thing else I
have seen of hers. I fancy she had some assistance in that article. How surprising it is
that Sully should mention so great a man as
D'Aubigné so seldom, and with such contempt! never taking notice of any of his ex-
ploits, and speaking of him as a man remarka-
ble only for sedition and slander! How constantly is great vanity accompanied by envy!
I always thought Sully abounded in the former,
but did not know before that he was so strongly tinctured by the latter. I do not condemn
Henry for not loving D'Aubigné; for certainly,
with all his great qualities, he was inexcusably
insolent to the king, and shewed no personal
regard for him, nor good will to monarchy.
His zeal was confined to the Huguenot party;
for I cannot place it all to the account of re-

ligion. Had the free exercise of that been all
they aimed at, the edict of Nantz would have
quieted them, and we should not have seen
D'Aubigné concurring in an attempt to re-
kindle the war which had so nearly destroyed
his country, as soon as the weakness of admi-
nistration afforded an opportunity for it. I
think him therefore no true patriot, though a
zealous religionist. His history is however
entertaining, and characters interesting. I
hope the work meets with applause in the
world.

LETTER LII.

Mill Hill, Nov. 30, 1772.

" It was not in a palace, my dear Mrs. Carter, but in my own little quiet dwelling, where
only I can read or think to any purpose, that
I got through five volumes of Lardner, who is
indeed the most tiresome writer I ever had to
do with; yet being very ignorant of ecclesi-
astical history, I met with some accounts of
the fathers, which entertained me, though the
extracts from their writings by no means

raised my veneration for their judgments.
What Lardner undertakes, is to prove that
the Gospels, Acts, and Epistles now canoni-
cal, were received by the earliest christians,
and reverenced as the writings of those whom
we ascribe them to. And that the spurious
ones which appeared after them were received
only by a few schismatics in the early ages.
Of this I think he produces sufficient testimony. The doctrine of immortality is a Gospel
of such glad tidings, that less evidence than
that of the Apostles would dispose one rea-
dily to receive it. Such wisdom is from
above; and God seems to raise up extraordinary lights in almost all countries at some season or other, to guide the human mind to some
of the great truths of morality, and to awaken
the hope of immortality. Amidst all the darkness I labour under, I trust in God this cheer-
ing view will never be taken from me; and
that I shall attain to a state of more information in a future life, if not in this.

" I suppose you read of Miss Ord's marriage in the papers. I had a letter not long

ago from Mrs. Ord, in which she speaks of
Mr. Bigge in the highest terms, and of her
daughter's happiness ; but very feelingly of
her own loss, which is indeed a severe one;
for I never saw a more amiable and perfect
friendship between a mother and daughter,
than subsists with them ; and to give up the
first place in the heart where one has gar-
nered up one's chief delight, to part with her
constant companionship, and to know that it
is in the power of another to carry her to ever
so great a distance, is what self-love must feel
in spite of generosity."

LETTER LIII.

Farnham Castle, July 20.

" I am much obliged by the kind interest
you take in the success of my publication,
which has indeed been far beyond my expectation. The bookseller is preparing a second
edition with all haste, the whole of the first being gone out of his hands, which, considering
that he printed off fifteen hundred at first, is an
extraordinary quick sale. I attribute this
success principally to Mrs. Montagu's name

and patronage, and secondly to the world's
being so fond of being educated, that every
book on that subject is well received. My
friends all fret and scold at me for having sold
my copy, and grudge poor Walter his profits.
But for my part I do not repent what I have
done, as I am persuaded the book would not
have prospered so well in my hands as in his.
Though I love money reasonably well, yet I
fear I have still more vanity than avarice, and
am therefore very happy in the approbation
the letters meet with, though my pockets are
not the heavier. I have had within these few
days a very kind long letter from Mrs. Montagu, with a very satisfactory account of the
improvement of her health, and of the success
of her truly laudable zeal for Dr. Beattie. I
am sincerely delighted to hear of the honour
he receives, and of the probability of his
sharing in more substantial rewards. What
delight must our admirable friend enjoy in the
power of raising merit into such lustre! Her
activity in its behalf is unequalled, and the noble use which she makes of that influence her
own celebrity gives her, entitles her to a much

higher praise, than even those talents to which she owes her power. She seems at present sincerely weary of the great world and its fatiguing homage, and heartily to enjoy repose and retirement. But the return of winter will awaken the relish of those pleasures, which are providentially annexed to such a shining but laborious course, as a fit spur to such a spirit as hers, to quit inglorious ease. I know of nothing harder to define than the limits of innocence in the love of praise. To condemn it entirely, seems to me unphilosophical and unjust; yet the danger of excess in it is so great, that it threatens to swallow up all real virtue. Tell me what you think on this subject, and how you have preserved your mind from vanity, amidst all that could gratify and inflame it? I am inclined to think that the love of praise, like all our natural passions, is in itself innocent, and only becomes criminal when it seeks gratification at the expence of duty. Whenever it in any way interferes with our love to God, or to our fellow creatures, it must cease to be innocent; but the difficulty is to know when it is so. I know you will refer me to Mrs. Talbot's excellent dialogue upon vanity ; but though I admire much of what she says upon it, she does not wholly satisfy me ; and I will not let you off from this discussion.

" You do not mention your health in your last, which, though in general it is construed into good news, does not satisfy from you, because I know how much you hate complaining. As you equally love to give pleasure, I rather fear your silence is a sign you had not a very good account to give of yourself. However, I desire always to have some account of your health, be it good or bad.

" My most earnest good wishes will ever attend you, for I am ever my dear Mrs. Carter's, &c."

LETTER LIV.

" I thank you, my dear Mrs. Carter, for your kind letter, and for complying with my request, by giving me your opinion on the subject of the love of praise. I am pleased to find that our sentiments agree perfectly. Moralists are too apt to deny to virtue the enjoyment of those pleasures, which providence meant to be her attendants, and a kind of foretaste of her rewards : so long as these pleasures are only the consequences, and not the motive of virtuous actions, all is safe. But I own I think there is great need to watch over the heart in this respect, lest the relish of them, as consequences, may degenerate into making them the end of our exertions."

LETTER LV.

" I am sorry you have suffered from the rheumatism, though I like it better in your foot than in your head. Were you ever suspected of the gout? Methinks it would be worth your while to be laid by the heels once a year, (as little as you like confinement) to be rid of the head ach and rheumatic pains for the rest of the year : therefore when you get it to your toes again, pray nurse it well, and encourage it with flannel. I had the pleasure of hearing from Mrs. Montagu a few days ago, and am happy to find that her health has not suffered by the affliction she has sustained. My friend Mr. Pepys, sent me a long and most affecting account of the death of good Lord Lyttelton, which has confirmed and increased my veneration and love for his character. Poor Mr. Pepys is a sincere mourner for him, but says he hopes to be the better man as long as he lives, for having been a witness of the last touching scene of his admirable friend.

" I have read through Hawksworth's Account of the Voyages of Cooke, &c. I mean as much of them as is readable, for the greater part is only so to navigators. 'Tis a melancholy kind of reading ! What an idea

does it give one of the state of near half the
Globe! and how hard is it to restrain one's
wishes to penetrate into the hidden counsels
of God, to find out the reason of so great a
part of the human species being left so destitute both of corporeal and intellectual good!
If the attainment of virtue and happiness is
the end of our being, how should it be that the
inhabitants of Otaheite have no consciousness
of evil, in the most detestable and pernicious
practices ? These are things that cannot but
excite my wonder, but I think they will never
shake my belief in an over-ruling Providence,
which is not merely speculative, but a sentiment that I seem to feel irresistibly. I think
nothing can be more injudicious than Hawksworth's discussion of that subject in his preface. To many it appears impious, but I
think his meaning is free from any irreligious
tendency; it however may hurt and unsettle
the principles of others, and was quite *hors
de place* in such a work. I don't think he has
gained credit by it in any respect, so he must
content himself with money. There is a very
small part of this large and expensive work

that affords the least entertainment, and some of the reflections and remarks of the author appear to me of very little value. Upon the whole I was, like every body else that I know, who has read the work, rather disappointed. Have you seen it ?"

LETTER LVI.

Wardour Street, Dec. 14.

" I am sorry the complaint in your foot turned to no better account. I am sure I have no malice to the poor dear foot, (for I love the ground it goes on,) other than in kindness to the head ; and if that can reap no profit by laying the other by the heels, e'en let the foot traverse the earth at pleasure. As to rheumatism, it belongs to us both. I am persuaded that whatever might originally have been the case in my face, rheumatism has at present a great share in it.

" Poor Doctor Hawksworth! His death happened at an ill time for his fame, and one cannot but wish it had pleased God to take him out of the world before he had cast a shade

on a reputation so very respectable as a moral
and religious writer. Many suppose that the
censures of the world occasioned his death;
but I am not very ready to believe in such kind
of causes, which are always assigned upon the
remotest probability.

" Mrs. R——'s death was undoubtedly
occasioned by the shock she received from
that of her daughter, who came to pay
her a morning visit, was taken with violent
fits, which flung her into labour, was brought
to bed at Parson's Green, and seemed in a
good way for a fortnight, when one night
Mrs. R—— was waked with the news that her
fits had returned, and that she was dying.—
The poor mother got up in time to see her
die, and immediately said she had taken her
death's wound, and should not long survive.
She died within a fortnight. Though the cir-
circumstance is so dreadful that one cannot
hear of it without being shocked, one can
scarce refrain from smiling at her will, in which
she has left particular directions to be buried
either on a Sunday or a Thursday. These

were her lucky days when living ; but I wonder what sort of luck she thought they would
bring her in the grave."

LETTER LVII.

June 15, 1777.

" Many thanks to you, my dear Mrs. Carter, for your most kind letter. I have been
very little at home since I received it, or should
have been quicker in my acknowledgments ;
for indeed the great pleasure it conveyed to
me, demanded them immediately. I hope
there is no harm in being exquisitely gratified
by the approbation you are so good as to express on a second reading of my little publi-
cations ; the hope which you confirm, of their
being capable of doing some good, has indeed
afforded me an inexpressible satisfaction,
which, as far as I know my own heart, is not
founded in vanity. It appeases in some measure, that uneasy sense of helplessness and in-
significancy in society, which has often depressed and afflicted me ; and gives me some
comfort with respect to the poor account I

can give of ' That one talent which is death
to hide.'

" The testimony of a friend, and particularly of such a friend, is far more precious
than that of the public voice, had it been even
as universal as you partially suppose; and is
laid up in the choicest cabinet of my heart,
along with every other endearing proof of your
friendship and goodness to me.

" I suppose you have heard a great deal of
the Abbé Reynal, who is in London. I fancy
you would have served him as Dr. Johnson did,
to whom when Mrs. Vesey introduced him, he
turned from him, and said he had read his
book and would have nothing to say to him.
I am told that his wit flows in an unceasing
torrent, and instead of ' spitting a pearl
every minute,' it is one continued chain of
pearls which issues from his mouth. I have
not been in the way to gather any of them. I
should like to see him as a spectacle, but
should no more desire his acquaintance than

Doctor Johnson, for there is an impertinence in French philosophy that turns my stomach."

LETTER LVIII.

Hadley, July 30.

" I am sorry, but not surprised, my dear Mrs. Carter, to find that your health has suffered by the strange unnatural behaviour of the elements this summer. It is more to be wondered at that I, who am usually as much affected by skyey influence as any body, have continued uncommonly well since I have been here; and the delightful society I am in, makes good amends for the want of those enjoyments which the weather precludes.

" The Abbé Reynal dined at Mrs. Boscawen's at Glanvilla, about ten days ago, and she was so obliging to ask Mrs. A. Burrows and me to meet him in the afternoon. I was exceedingly entertained, and not a little amazed, (notwithstanding all I had heard about him) by the unceasing torrent of wit and stories, not unmixed with good sense, which

flowed from him; he had held on at the same
rate from one at noon, (when he arrived at
Glanvilla) and we heard that he went the same
evening to Mrs. Montagu's, in Hill Street,
and kept on his speed till one in the morning.
In the hour and half I was in his company,
he uttered as much as would have made him
an agreeable companion for a week, had he
allowed time for answers. You see such a
person can only be pleasing as a thing to wonder at once or twice. His conversation was,
however, perfectly inoffensive, which is more
than his writings promise; his vivacity, and
the vehemence of his action, (which, however, had not any visible connexion with his discourse) were amusing to me, who am little
accustomed to foreigners. Mrs. Boscawen is
a very good neighbour to us here, and a most
delightful companion every where. I never
knew her in finer spirits than of late. One
could not but make a comparison much to her
advantage, between the overwhelming display
of the abbé's talents, and that natural, polite,
and easy flow of wit and humour which en-
livens her conversation."

LETTER LIX.

Old Alresford, Hants.

" My dear Mrs. Carter's long-lost letter did at last come to my hands, very dirty on the outside, but very elegant in the inward and intellectual part. I know I have no chance of another till I have duly and truly paid my thanks for this; therefore I need no other motive for following my letter to Miss S—— with another to you. But moreover I know you will both be glad to hear that my dreaded journey is got over without any disaster, and that neither of us poor old infirm mortals failed in the way. As to my aunt, she behaved the best of the two upon the road, where, to my sorrow, we spent three times as many hours as were necessary, because she chose to go in a hired chariot, with the same horses, and sleep on the road; but I took Pamela with me, (which I had not read since my enthusiasm for the author,) and screamed it in her ears as much as my lungs would permit. I must own it appeared somewhat different from what I thought of it thirty years ago; yet I still see, in each of Richardson's works, amazing genius, unpolished indeed, either by learning or knowledge of polite life, but making its way to the heart by strokes of nature that perhaps would have been lost, or at least weakened, by the restraints of critical elegance. It is only from the ignorant that we can now have any thing original; every master copies from those that are of established authority, and does not look at the natural object.

" I am now in a very pleasant place, and a fine air, and endeavour to keep up those walking powers which I felt so proud of at S. Lodge, that I was disappointed because you would not admire them. I am within nine miles of my brother John, who yesterday brought my niece to see me. I was in hopes to have gone to them at Meonstoke in a fortnight, but fear I must stay longer here, though nature draws me strongly to my own. I long for a history of all your travels and adventures since I saw you, and a very particular description of all that relates to the friends you are with;

characters so interesting that one wishes to be
acquainted with their very pigsty. They are
indeed respectable in the proper use of the
word; which I agree with you is very ill applied to the Abbé Reynal, unless confined to
his abilities merely, exclusive of the use he
makes of them. And even his understanding
is so clouded by vanity and coxcombicality,
that it often excites my laughter instead of my
admiration. In his pathetic rhapsodies in
praise of incontinence, and in reverence of the
blessed institution of a public brothel adjoining
to the Temple, he is most truly ridiculous, as
well as immoral. I abhor, as much as he can
do, that gloomy superstition which would strip
life of its sweetest comforts and dearest chari-
ties. I have as high honour and reverence for
the institution of marriage as Milton has, but
how that of promiscuous prostitution can re-
dound to the glory of God, or the good of
mankind, it belongs to French philosophy to
point out."

LETTER LX.

Wardour Street, Nov. 1782.

" I have read through the three volumes of Trembley that you were so good to lend me, which I found to be no small undertaking. He is a very verbose writer, and the manner of dividing his work into discourses occasions endless recapitulations and repetitions. If it were shorter, and more simple, (for I must own I think it has more eloquence than does it good) it would be a very good book for the purpose designed—that of instructing young people, with whom difficulties are not to be supposed, or may be glossed over easily ; but I cannot say it answered my purposes, or threw any new light upon my mind. I am pleased with the temper of the man, and the benevolence and moderation of his principles ; but, like all rationalists, he gives the sense he thinks most reasonable, let the words of Scripture be ever so refractory. Every sect of Christians may find texts that suit them ; and none of them trouble themselves about making the said texts

agree with each other : however, the moral precepts, thank God, are plain enough, and if I
could but live up to them, I should not fear
to have incurred any guilt by the unavoidable
suggestions of the very imperfect reason God
has given me, and should hold fast the blessed
hope of everlasting life, though all the priests,
or even apostles, that ever lived should ana-
thematise me. Trembley is not one of those
that are inclined to do so, but lays the stress
where it ought to be laid, on the genuine merits
of christianity, charity, and good living.

" Pray, my dear Mrs. Carter, have you read
Cecilia ? I do not remember to have heard
your opinion of it, but I find with great pleasure that Mrs. Montagu (who was not very favourable to Evelina) is warm in her commen-
dations of this book. I am fond of Miss Bur-
ney, and delighted with her works. There
was one charm in Evelina, which to me sur-
passed even every thing in Cecilia; this was
the just and natural picture of the purest and
most elegant love. Lord Orville and Evelina
are lovers after my own heart. Mrs. Montagu,

entre nous, is an ignoramus on this subject, as
I have observed on many occasions, nor are
you quite an adept. It is the only subject in
the world of which I think myself a better judge
than either of you. The morality of both
works is uncommonly perfect, and shews an
admirable rectitude of mind in the writer.—
There is in Cecilia much useful satire, much
entertainment, and a force of pathos that was
really too much for me. Perhaps there is too
great a number of characters, but most of them
are surprisingly well drawn, and kept up with
admirable consistency. But I did not mean to
say so much of my own opinion, when I only
wanted to know yours. I have begun to dip
into poor Rousseau's posthumous works, which
are most melancholy reading, as they shew
the most evident madness, and that of the most
miserable and afflicting kind : he believed all
Europe in a combination against him, and that
the plots of his enemies had rendered him so
much the contempt and abhorrence of mankind, that the very beggars would throw his
alms in his face. In the midst of this distrac-
tion he often writes finely. His imagination,

which tortured him with so many unreal evils, made him, however, some amends, by transporting him, whenever he was alone, into an ideal world, where he made for himself such a society as he liked, and found all those blessings this world denied him. The liveliness of his fancy made these reveries a real happiness, which he says he enjoyed four or five hours in every day. I hope they do not infer madness, for I own this is one of my resources when the world refuses me materials for that happiness which my nature incessantly desires ; but I dare not deliver myself up to it as entirely as he did, lest it should disqualify me for real life."

LETTER LXI.

London, June, 1783.

" I had yesterday the pleasure of seeing Mrs. D—— better, though still lame, and Dr. D—— pretty well recovered. I am concerned to think of the distress they must have been in when both so ill at the same time. What sad sufferers they are in their health! and how

continually is human happiness defeated by
the infirmities of the body. I am persuaded
there must be something very wrong and unnatural in the method of living in civilized
countries ; for it could never be the original
nature of the animal man to be so perpetually
infested by disease. Perhaps we ought not to
have eat animal food ; and perhaps all that con-
tributes to cultivate our finer sensations, and
even all that adorns and ennobles our minds,
may tend to render our bodies delicate and
liable to perpetual injury. Somebody was ob-
serving, t'other day, that love was of modern
invention, and that no such thing existed in
Homer's time. Nervous complaints, I dare
say, came into fashion with love, and brought
a great many more painful feelings in their
train. However, I am better pleased to have
been all my life a sufferer from them, than to
have been carrying stinking seal, with a blan-
ket skewered round me, into the woods after
some lordly savage, perfectly unacquainted
with the fashion of love or conversation."

LETTER LXII.

June, 1784

" You were very good, my dear Mrs. Carter, to favour me with a letter so early ; and
upon the whole the account it brought me
was as satisfactory as I could expect. I should
have thanked you for it sooner but that I have
been very much indisposed this last fortnight.
A bad cold brought back my cough and low
fever, with the addition of a sore throat. The
dejection of spirits which attended the low
fever is by much the worst part of the disorder ; and you well know that one symptom
of it is a perfect listlessness and disinclination
to set about any employment that can be
omitted. I am better, but still far from well :
however I have just enough power of exertion
to resolve that I will no longer appear ungrateful to your kind attention. I do not expect to get rid of my complaints whilst this
watery solstice continues. Sunshine is essential to my well being, and when to that is

added country air, I flatter myself I shall be restored to my common state of health, which, I bless God, is such as affords me many enjoyments. I am sorry for your poor friend Mrs. ——; such imaginary distempers, are real miseries, and not the less to be pitied for not shortening a life which they render perfectly uncomfortable. I think there is hardly a stronger argument for a future state of retribution, than may be drawn from the existence of those complaints which affect the mind as well as the body, and in which reason and virtue are utterly incapable of giving support or comfort. Our enjoyments in this world seem to depend more on animal spirits than on principle or right conduct; and a wicked man, with high health and spirits, shall laugh through the day, whilst an innocent and pious mind is drooping under the heaviest dejection, and more alarmed by mere human frailties, than the first is by shocking crimes. The consequence I draw from this is highly consolatory and delightful, for " That which God delights in must be happy."

I have not been able to wait on Mrs. ——, who, I suppose, has now left London some days. I am sorry to hear that she is uneasy on account of her amiable friend, Miss ——, who, it seems, is about to commit the heinous sin of marrying a clergyman that has only a small living. As you know my way of thinking on such subjects, you will not suspect me of condemning her. The situation she was in with Mrs. ——, is, of all others, the least favourable to matrimony. Men of small pretentions would not look up to her, and men of great ones would look above her. In effect the experiment has been tried for ten years, and every year makes the chance considerably worse. What then was more natural, or indeed more reasonable, than to lower her views, and accept a man she likes, a gentleman and a man of character, (for this I presume is the case, as I have heard nothing suggested to the contrary), with the prospect of living on a narrow income? And what have her friends to do on the occasion but to assist her as far as they can, to make out a reasonable competence? I hope Mrs. ——'s displeasure will

not affect her intentions of benefiting her
adopted daughter; for had she been her real
daughter, at her time of life, it can hardly be
disputed that she had a right to judge for herself, and has not forfeited any claim to kindness
by seeking her own happiness in a lawful, and
(in rank and education) not unsuitable marriage.

LETTER LXIII.

London, November, 1797.

" I have been returned to town about a
fortnight, after spending two months with my
friend Mrs. Ogle, at the Deanery of Winchester. I could not there reckon myself in the
country, which I enjoyed only during the few
weeks I was at Hadley. But never was a
summer and autumn in which one had so little
reason to regret being surrounded with brick
and tile; and my good friend carried me an
airing every tolerable day, which helped my
health, though I cannot boast of it much. I
brought a bad cold with me to town, which the

fogs and cold will not suffer to get well.—
Otherwise I think my general health is better
than it was some months ago, and indeed as
well as I ought to expect, considering that
with so many complaints I have attained the
age of man.

" It was a great pleasure to me to receive
a comfortable account from yourself, which
has since been confirmed to me from different
hands ; amongst the rest from Mrs. J. Pitt,
whom I had the pleasure of seeing at Winchester. She was esteemed a great acquisition to that town, where I hope, for the sake
of my friends there, she means to return ; but
she left it before I did. She is still lovely, in
person as in mind.

" I had great satisfaction in seeing my
darling niece established in the happiest manner at Winchester with a husband who seems
in every respect calculated to make her happy. My younger niece was on a visit to Mrs.
Ogle the whole time I was there, and we tra-
velled to London together. I found her in

poor health and bad spirits; for the loss of her brother* affected her so deeply that I almost feared she would sink under it. And it was long before she regained any degree of cheerfulness; but I bless God she is now recovered in health, and much mended in spirits.

" I was pleased to hear that you, as well as my dear Mrs. Burrows, were able to pursue the pleasant and healthful employment of a gardener. She worked very hard whilst I was with her, and though she cannot do the same in this season, she assures me she has preserved a good share of health through all the bad weather. I was also well pleased that you were no longer reduced to seek amusement only in novels. I have surfeited upon them and am 'supt full of horrors.' Can you tell me of something rather more rational without being too deep for a feeble brain ? I suppose you have read (for every body has) ' Pursuits of Literature ;' and have felt the same

* Captain William Mulso, Royal Navy, who was lost in the Hermes sloop, with all his crew, January, 1797.

indignation I did at the author, for making a she dog of Mrs. Montagu. And the same contempt for his taste, his spleen, envy, and nonsense, in that line which displays them all.

" Her yelp, though feeble, and her sandals blue."

A she dog in sandals is not more absurd than a feeble yelp applied to one of the ablest as well as most ingenious criticisms that ever was written. Indisposed as I was against the author, by this and some other instances of ill nature, I cannot but acknowledge that some of his notes and prefaces testify a laudable zeal on the right side both in politics and religion, which should mollify our resentment against his scurrility and indecency.— Poor Doctor Warton is severely dealt with: how far he deserves it I know not, for I have not seen his last publication, but should be grieved if he had disgraced his later years by any thing like what this coarse satirist alledges. I suppose nobody knows who he is. The secret seems well kept, and with reason, for he has great cause to dread the vengeance of so many wounded without provocation.

" My little world are gathering fast together; but, alas, in winter I am usually cooped
up, and can seldom see them. I hope you
will not fail us after Christmas, and that fate
will be more propitious to our meetings than
last year, but whether in presence or absence,
I must be ever my dear Mrs. Carter's affectionate and obliged friend,

H. CHAPONE."

END OF THE FIRST VOLUME.

WRIGHT, Printer, St. John's Square.

For EU product safety concerns, contact us at Calle de José Abascal, 56–1°, 28003 Madrid, Spain or eugpsr@cambridge.org.

.

 www.ingramcontent.com/pod-product-compliance
Ingram Content Group UK Ltd.
Pitfield, Milton Keynes, MK11 3LW, UK
UKHW012346130625
459647UK00009B/568